AND STILL I SMILE

AND STILL I SMILE

An Optimist's Guide to Life, Fitness,
and Higher Wisdom

Leigh Hickombottom

Shesique Publications
Orlando, Florida

To the four beauties of my life:
You are my world and the magic behind life's beautiful moments. Thank you for inspiring me and reminding me that receiving love is just as important as giving it. I love you all. Be the change this world needs in each of your unique ways.

To my parents:
Thank you for bringing me into this world and giving me a great life filled with the opportunities of love, a solid foundation, and the ability to choose my experiences.

CONTENTS

PREFACE

I feel as though I have written this book before and I am rewriting it. This is the tale of the life I was always meant to live. I was born to heal, love, create, and live my passion out loud. I am a consciously aware woman, born Patrice, now known as Leigh, Hickombottom.

What you see of me in print or social media are tiny glimpses of who I am. Although this book won't show you everything about me, it will teach you more than you have known during the years of my fitness career. It will show you more about me than anyone has seen. In this memoir, you will gain insights on my vulnerabilities and learn why the girl behind the photographs smiles as she does today.

Life is a miraculous journey. I want to show you mine through my own eyes. So please take a walk with me as I journey back to the major pains in my life and the important lessons I learned from them. Inside, I am still a delicate girl though I have the power of a goddess. Like so many others, I have lived through harsh experiences. I have endured, and I have overcome. I will share with you what I have learned about how to live more through your own experiences and see the beauty in each moment.

You need never get lost in a moment, as with each thought and action you create your experience. On a small scale, what you do and think affects you. On a grander scale, your actions affect an entire world. Each of us came into life prepared with all the tools we need to accomplish our goals. We are each given the strength to remember who we are and to serve humanity. We are born, not as victims, but as warriors of light. We possess the power of deeper understanding, of conscious creation. From the level of understanding the power of different energy vibrations we can heal ourselves and the world, one person at a time, one plant at a time, and one animal at a time.

The greatest gifts you can take from the material you are about to read are mastery of self-love and knowledge of your connection to everything that has ever existed or ever will exist. You will come to see that the journey has always been about going within. It is from here that we are connected to, and manifesting from the universal and nonjudgmental love of God/Source. You are the pure essence of God in a human form. Embrace all that you are in this moment and each experience that has brought you to your current state of being. On top of that, know that you can be even more. You are greater than you have ever imagined. Journey with me and see life through my eyes as a consciously aware, multidimensional being of light.

I am only an example of many different perspectives. So before you begin to read these chapters about my life and achievements and about how to achieve your own desires, open your heart, as well as your imagination, to the unlimited vibration of unconditional love and oneness that we are. Choose in this moment to believe that everything is possible and every person, place, and thing you have ever come into contact with has led you closer to the truth of you. With your heart wide open, breathe deeply in and out seven times.

Now begin reading perhaps the longest meditation ever written to help heal those aspects of your being that you believe are flawed. This book is written at the highest vibration that exists: the vibration of unconditional love. It is written for the highest good of all and for the purpose of bringing us back into the state of oneness.

We all have a journey to take in life. We can scream and kick in resistance to it, or we can smile. I choose to smile. We never know the story of another's life until he or she shares it with us. In this book I present you with a bit of my story. May my words inspire your journey. May you be open enough to see what you have in each moment as a gift and grateful enough for all of what you have gone through, which in the end left you smiling still.

Light and Love,

Leigh Hickombottom

PART ONE

MY LIFE STORY

CHAPTER 1

WORLD, HERE I AM

This is where I begin to humanize the image of Leigh Hickombottom that you have seen on the Internet or in magazines. This is where you will begin to see the reason why I still smile today. My hope is that by the time you have finished reading my story, you'll have more than just the images, quotes, and words of inspiration that accompany my public persona.

I was born in the state of Mississippi, the elder of fraternal twins. Though my parents moved us to Texas when I was still an infant, Mississippi was where I started out. I won't say life was easy for me back then, but I am nonetheless grateful today for my early experiences. I started off kicking and screaming, ready to get out of my mother's belly a few months early due to environmental confinement: My twin brother was taking up most of the space. I was so ready to be in this world that out I came regardless of the doctor's prescribed due date.

My mother developed complications and was told that one of the children might not survive labor. The doctors asked my father who he would choose to save if there was a choice between us babies and our mother. I don't know what his answer was, but I must have heard the question and been so determined to show what was possible that I was the first one born, heart beating and determined to live.

For the next few weeks, I lived behind hospital walls as the staff helped me to get strong enough for the real world. My twin brother, on the other hand, went home after only a week. I was left in the hands of strangers and my life depended on their services. Looking back, it was my drive to succeed and do what I came here to do for humanity that strengthened me and helped me pull through. There I was, fresh in the world and already having setbacks: being told by others what was and was not possible for me. But here I am today, breathing on my own, with no developmental problems or impediments, a testament to what is possible.

I came into this world told I was too weak to survive due to only partially formed organs and other issues many premature babies have to deal with. The smile that I developed early and maintain to this day began when I left the hospital and came home to my family. I thrived when doctors and nurses thought I would fail. If that is not something to smile about then I don't know what is. That is the spirit of a warrior, and a lesson not to let limiting beliefs or knowledge defeat the power of a spirit that is blessed by the light of God/Source.

My brother and I were blessed to have parents who left college with masters' degrees and had very successful careers. My parents had two different personalities from which we were to select our own character building choices. My mother was a strict, loving, and God-fearing woman who, in my eyes, was a bit controlling. She loved to shop. Though I knew she loved me, I felt I was not her favorite twin. As a child, I could not understand why she favored my brother and assumed it was because he resembled her in skin tone, hair texture, and eyes. He was a boy, and maybe this was what she desired most. Feeling rejected by my mother, I quickly became a daddy's girl. This is where I felt most loved.

My father had a positive outlook on life. He was an honest, athletic man, always smiling and laughing, the definition of a people person. He had a love of the ocean that he passed down to me. I can remember going into his office, infatuated with the model sailboat on his desk. I loved it. It always took me away. My thoughts became the melody of the ocean near this miniature sailboat. I was nourished by my father's devoted time to me and his support as he cheered me on in life.

Moving through the years of my life, we come to an important and confusing time for me: my toddler years. In that early stage would come my second harsh reality—with the first being my premature birth. As a toddler, I was still too young to go to school and had two hardworking parents who worked full-time jobs. This meant a roof over my head, great big meals, and my parents still married happily and loving me. This also meant that my time and safety were

entrusted to a babysitter who turned out to be neither re-
sponsible, nor moral. Nor was her sibling, who molested me
with her knowledge. How could someone take advantage of
a tiny child? What kind of world was I living in? It was a level
of abuse totally foreign to me. Having never been exposed
to sexual violence, all I knew was that it was wrong.

I was forced to return to my babysitter, even though I did
not want to for obvious reasons. This was my first experience of lacking trust in people, especially adults. While I will
not go into the details of my abuse, as I feel it is unneces-
sary, I will say that it has taken a lifetime to heal and forgive
such deep hurt. You might be wondering if I told my parents
what was happening. I told the one person I trusted the
most, my father. Twice I communicated this trauma to him;
once as a child and once as a teen, and all I remember is
silence. I felt his silence was due to shock, fear, and hurt
over what was done to his child.

My parents eventually pulled away from this sitter and
the remainder of my toddler years continued without major
incidents, just a couple of minor scrapes and a whole lot
of play. I did feel hesitation towards opening up or playing
around adults, but I still smiled. I made sure I was always
around my brother, attached to his hip. We were close sib-
lings during the toddler years. He was my best buddy and
he loved to play with my toys. I was a bit of a tomboy, and I
loved cars and playing in the dirt. I did like dolls as well, but
the other play was much more fun.

As I reflect back on it now, how good it was to be so
young and carefree.

CHAPTER 2

SCHOOLING YEARS

During my early years in school, my parents provided me with a great education and a foundation for believing in things unseen. For me this meant belief in such beings as God, whom today I call Source, in addition to a whole realm of angels, fairies, and beautiful spirits who walked the earth: Jesus, Buddha, and Quan Yin. We will get into all of this later.

My brother and I were fortunate: We had parents who encouraged us to explore athletics and the creative arts throughout all of our schooling. My mother danced and played the flute when she was younger. My father has always been an athlete. In school he participated in a range of sports from tennis to football. Today, this amazing and wonderful man runs marathons, plays golf, mountain bikes, hikes, and practices yoga. Needless to say, we were very active kids, always playing outdoors, participating actively in sports, going to the beach, camping, and more. I think my parent's goal was for us to find our niches in our daily lives while staying active. I also think it was done to balance our extracurricular activities with our studies, helping us to build a balanced character. As a child, these outlets felt rewarding to me after the hard studies of schooling and the use of the logical mind.

Five years of my schooling were spent in private school and the rest spent in the public educational system. Beginning around the fourth grade, I attempted my first series of extracurricular events. I played soccer, basketball, and volleyball for my school. Though I loved playing volleyball, I really did not thrive in any of these sports. I also took up tennis alongside my brother for a while and loved it. I was very competitive with my twin. I wanted to excel and advance to more challenging lessons before him. However, my brother proved excellent at tennis, advancing quickly in lessons and tournaments state wide. While I loved playing, I was frustrated with my brother's better skill, and ultimately quit. I remained involved, cheering my brother on as he continued playing until the end of high school. I spent many years traveling all over Texas to watch my brother compete and excel in his sport of choice.

During these same years, I tested out a few different forms of creative art. I first took up dance, through ballet and jazz. I started with jazz dance and realized quickly that this was not for me. The movements seemed too fast. At the time, I was looking for grace and harmony in my art and both my observation of and experience with jazz dance left it lacking.

I quickly picked up ballet, which was more my pace. Today I still consider it to be one of the most beautiful forms of moving art. My initial experiences with ballet, first as an ob-server, then as a practicing student, left me amazed. Ballet incorporated the graceful movement of music I had been searching for. It was music flowing through the body. At the time I saw the grace that existed there. Now I know that it is the body and music fluidly merging as one that create its beauty. While I never performed ballet live on stage, I did gain something by the time I stopped studying it that would prove invaluable to me. With both of these forms of art I realized something: There was, for each, an ideal body that epitomized the art. Even at that early age I was intrigued by what I consider eloquent bodies. I knew this eloquence was what I wanted to bring about in my own body.

Leaving the dance behind, I quickly jumped into playing the piano. This lasted about three months—another short-lived activity. Yet I learned another lesson. I learned about my love for music. The piano produced a relaxing and mesmer-izing sound. As a very busy child both mentally and phys-ically, this one activity kept me in a calm, almost peaceful state. Not to mention that I admired the grace and poise my piano teacher possessed when she played the piano and moved about. Her aura was graceful and warm. I loved this about her and desired to emulate the beauty of character I observed in her presence.

If we fast-forward to seventh grade, we will see me find my ideal sport: track. I fell in love instantly. We raced during physical education (PE) periodically and I learned I was gift-ed with speed. The coach asked me to run track for the school and I happily agreed. I already loved being outdoors and staying active. When coach asked me to run for the school it was an automatic, without hesitation, yes. From that moment on I was hooked.

Track was not just a sport to me. Like a finely painted masterpiece to a painter, so to me was track. It was freeing, an expression of the beauty of the human physique eloquently merging with nature, artistically and vividly moving in forward motion. Running track was like falling in love with myself while trying to outrun the wind. This was for me.

That same year I started taking a Drama/Theater Arts class. Though I thought of myself as a social butterfly, this class was quite scary, yet invigorating. I truly enjoyed interacting with friends, but this was different. I would have to be willing to stand alone with all eyes on me at some point. Not to mention the pressure of memorizing my lines. Words flew out of my mouth easily outside of class, with friends and playing around in groups, even one on one. This class would prove challenging for me, and my first fear was revealed: fear of exposure.

Thus, I fell in love with yet another form of creative art, acting. This was using spoken words, actions, and emotions to magically engulf those watching. While I never took the stage due to fear, I did act in class for the remainder of high school.

Take note of three words you will see three times in this story. They are a staple to the person I am today. The first school I attended, from pre-K to first grade, was Most Precious Blood, which was located right outside of Houston, Texas. I should have loved it, but what I felt was just the opposite. We all wore horrible green uniforms and I had teachers who didn't understand my greatness. I had a very quick mouth, which I used to speak against things I didn't believe in, or to stand up for my best friend, my brother. I remember standing up for my twin against some bully. I got into trouble for helping my brother, whereas the bully was just told to sit down. I was blown away. This was from a teacher who felt I was being a problem child, in a school where there were a limited number of children of color, like me and my brother.

This teacher told me to sit down outside the classroom door, at the timeout desk. I did not. I felt I had done nothing wrong, and therefore should not abide by the teacher's request. She asked me again to go outside and sit at the desk. I went outside by choice this time; I was so frustrated at what I considered injustice from every angle from this woman. But I did not sit at that desk, I stood. I could see the teacher getting as frustrated with me as I was with her. She went back inside and began her class all over again, but this time I was making my presence known through the little rectangle window on the door. I was peeking in, looking with disgust at the bully as he first smiled at me in victory, then looked at the teacher with anger and hurt.

The teacher opened the door and requested again that I sit at the desk, saying that if I did not sit she would send me to principal's office. In response, I stood on the desk and was promptly sent to principal's office with a pink slip. I gladly walked there, ready to share tales of of the injustice with a reasonable adult. In short, I was told I had to follow rules even if I did not agree with them. However, the principal did side with me after hearing my version of the story.

When I returned to class, I was a lot calmer. Being able to explain my side of story, and having an adult acknowledge my feelings pacified me.

From Houston, my family moved further south in Texas and my brother and I attended public school for the next two years. In third grade, we had a Physical Education class that was my favorite class that year. The coach was a big, round, black man who weighed a solid 290 pounds and reminded me of one of the most important men who would ever enter my life: my papa, Joseph Quinn. Coach Hall was a big kid at heart and all the other kids loved being around him. He was our key to freedom from the monotony of the enclosed rooms we had to endure to get a better education.

On a warm, sunny day, the coach said we would be playing dodgeball. I loved playing this game because I was good at it and it required you to be quick on your feet. That day the coach joined in the game on my team, standing right next to me. Let the game begin! We played and soon, I was out of the game. It wasn't because I did not catch or dodge the ball, but because my coach was so into the game that when the ball came in our direction he accidentally stepped on my foot, falling down and using my face for a cushion. All 290 pounds of him rested on my eight-year-old skull. I remember being out of it, and not knowing how I got to the nurse's office. When I regained consciousness, it was not to the sight of my parents, who were speeding up to the school, but to the sight of my coach laughing as the nurse dislodged pebbles from the side of my face. The coach and other office staff were conversing about what happened. The only sound I remember was him laughing.

How dare the coach laugh about something so painful and serious? I had a waterfall of tears rolling down my face, blood gushing from the left side of my temple, and a throbbing head. I shut down and went into my own lonesome world. The faces and sounds disappeared as I felt I was in a big white room sitting on a chair in seclusion. I don't know where I drifted to, but if you could feel your soul leave the body, that is what I felt: not in totality, but partially, and I regained a more aware consciousness when my parents arrived.

My parents drove me to the emergency entrance of the hospital and the only thing I remember of the incident was leaving the ER with stitches. The coach, who was my favorite teacher at that school, never apologized. He was told by the school that he was no longer allowed to participate in activities with students beyond monitoring them. I left that school at the end of the school year.

Fourth through sixth grades I was back at private school, Most Precious Blood in Corpus Christi, Texas, where I would happily remain until the end of high school. Translated from Latin *Corpus Christi* means "body of Christ." I loved the years in Corpus Christi for a number of reasons. First, because I always had access to the ocean, and this city, located on the Gulf of Mexico, was where my intuitive gifts and connection to higher spiritual planes were born. Second, because I was grateful to return to Most Precious Blood for more schooling. The school settled me and gave me a good grounding.

Throughout the years spent here, I began to question what I was being taught about God. By the end of sixth grade, I had developed my own relationship with Source. I was blessed to have diverse teachers; all were totally different in looks and personality. My fourth grade teacher was a bit strict. She spoke British English with a strong accent and was a brunette. My fifth grade teacher was of thicker build, a blond, and held a strong southern accent. My sixth grade teacher was a red head with glasses; kind, but all business. Every day we would learn about Catholic religious beliefs or history, as well as academics. We would have to go to the church, which was on the same property, and sing or practice for the weekly service we had to attend during school. This service was in addition to the service I had to attend every Sunday morning with my family. Sometimes a small group of us would pray together for something, and I noticed that the prayer would work in my life.

I learned about Archangel Michael and found that he was always at my side. He has never left me since. I did not develop a connection with Archangel Michael early on. I simply knew he was around me and openly accepted his presence. I felt an urge and need to heal others, but I had a mental dilemma that was tugging away at me, conflicting with my heart's truth.

You see, I listened to the stories, rules, and lessons about God and Jesus I was being told, but I could not understand how God could cause harm or desire for another to live in pain. Why were we being taught to fear God when my experience was so positive in my connection with God? Jesus had walked our great Earth making miracles happen daily, and if the Bible was true, he had said we could do this, too, yet we were being taught that only Jesus, God's son, could perform such astonishing miracles. This baffled me. So I listened and silently held reservations on the beliefs we were taught.

The church seemed full of judgment and collection baskets, which they upgraded to envelopes with our names on them as we got older in order to keep tabs on who was donating. I did not feel as if it was a true gift to donate because they expected it on top of the tuition my parents paid for me to attend the school. What Jesus and God did was for free.

My dilemma grew.

By the sixth grade the school completed a new church and chapel area with a beautiful gold dome and sanctuary. This is still the most beautiful catholic church I've ever stepped foot in. Some days when I needed to talk to God about my life, I would go to the chapel alone and pour my heart out, ask for help with things, just sit, and be in the presence of God's house.

During the final weekend of sixth grade, I went to this chapel for the last time I would until the baptism of my eldest daughter. I walked through the clear glass doors where there was an open area of different statues, one of Mother Mary among them, and I touched her feet in sadness of leaving a place that, though I was torn with beliefs, felt so like home to my heart. I proceeded, heavyhearted, through the large, wooden double doors of the chapel, walked to the third row of pews, and sat for a moment, staring at all the beautiful stained glass windows as the light shone through them.

As I sat in a pew, I reflected on the stories of Jesus and the important parts of his life that were depicted by different windows in the chapel. Then I turned my head back towards the front, to gaze at the monstrance, home to the Holy Eucharist, bowed my head in tears, and began to talk to God. I cried and acknowledged that God knew my heart and pleaded with him to bless me with the ability to heal people any way I could. I said, "I know I came here to heal the world, so please, bless me now." My eyes flooded with tears that showered my face with the holy water of my soul's release, as I pleaded to be blessed on this mission. As I did, I felt love of God fill my entire being. In my mind's eye, I saw a cylinder of pure, bright, white light flowing through and around me.

As I opened my hands and looked at them, they appeared to glow vividly green. What I saw was not in my mind, I was seeing it with my open eyes. Needless to say, at this age I was so scared, shocked, and excited all at once that it disrupted my flow of tears for an instant. I then cried in gratitude, sensing that God and angels were around me. My wish had instantaneously been granted. I went out of the chapel that day with my head held high, knowing that I would bless others through my touch and presence in the same way that God and Jesus had blessed me.

When it was time for junior high school, I was placed back in the public school system happy and ready for new experiences. Seventh and eighth grades were spent in a much larger building, where it seemed like there where hundreds of kids compared to my small classes in private school. I loved the size of the school. I met great people there, including a pair of cool sisters with awesome names. They were named after wines. Cab (Cabernet) was at my school while her sister, Chablis, was in the high school.

I made another friend there, Jessica, who was as pure a Texan as I had ever seen. With her long, blond hair and blue eyes, from head to toe she was pure cowgirl in every way. I loved hanging out with her!

In addition to friendships, junior high school gave me my first opportunity to participate in a sport: track. Track was my element. I felt wide open emotionally when I was running in and against the wind, honing fast movements, and training with weights under the guidance of a super cool coach.

During those two years, life was a breeze as far as school went, with the exception of math class. I had a very young teacher, a brunette with a long nose and a chip on her shoulder. This chip only seemed aimed at kids of my skin tone. Needless to say, she was not friendly and already seemed burned out from teaching though she was a young woman. One day during class, I was talking to a classmate. The teacher must have been in a poor mood, as she proceeded to yell at me about not talking while she is teaching. Her elevated voice did not help me receive her message at all. You see, though I agree I shouldn't have been talking in class, I felt that I didn't need to be reprimanded by a screaming, disgruntled employee of the school. So I spoke back.

My teacher took me outside into the hallway and belittled me with her harsh words while I cried. I couldn't look her in her eyes as I felt she did not deserve to look in mine.

Her harsh approach and words were unsatisfactory for any teacher to use with a student. She even grabbed my face and told me to look her in the eyes while she spoke, forcibly turning my face upward so my eyes could connect with hers. I looked in them and felt so much anger and hatred from her that I shut my eyes, and heard not one word of what she said after that. I went back inside and never again spoke to her or in her class. I made it through junior high with the support of some great people—she was not one of them.

I made it into the best high school in Corpus Christi: "Home of the Tigers, shining my colors blue and white." I met a variety of great people there. During freshman year, my parents thought I was in a rebellious stage because I was dating a man already out of high school. They tried to talk me out of it, but could not prevent us from seeing each other. I developed a bit of an attitude with my family and did not abide by a few of their rules. In my head, I was already an adult.

One day, out of the blue, my parents drove me to a scary-looking building. I asked my father where we were and what we were doing there, and he explained that I was going to speak to a woman about my problems. Alarm bells going off in my head, I yelled, "A psychiatrist!" Of course, I was right. I walked into the cold, jail-like building and noticed that the only beauty I saw was back the way I had come. Back outside there was greenery.

As we waited in the reception area, my dad signed a couple of papers and I sat in fear of where I was and what was happening. Then a lady walked out and greeted us, talking briefly before giving us a tour of the entire property. I kept looking at my father as we walked, trying to figure out what was going on and what it was he was not telling me. The tour completed I was told I would be staying there for a few days. I was devastated and cried, as this was a place for kids with serious problems, not just a rebellious teen acting up or not listening. Looking at my dad, I asked him why and for how long. I remember shaking in my skin. He promised me it was just for a few days and I felt a little more at ease.

I knew I did not need psychologists and detainment. I needed love and was not going to get it from this type of facility. My dad tried to soothe me. I knew he felt my pain and could not bear to see me cry, but this was all he could do. This was his way of trying to help. I understood, kissed my dad, and watched him leave.

For a few days, I endured psychological tests while being boarded with kids really in need of psychiatric assistance for many different reasons. I observed them every day and heard them speaking of suicide, drugs, and more. I was scared and felt all alone being left in the care of people I believed I could not trust. Those few days passed like years trapped in a haunted house. When my dad came back, I was excited to see him. His was a familiar face and it meant I was going back home! But my father told me I would be staying for another few days. I cried softly and looked him in the eyes as my heart hardened and crumbled to pieces.

I do not know if the extension of my stay was my father's choice or the hospital's, though I was sure I was the only

normal kid in there. I felt the administrators were just trying to make more money and that my dad was trusting the
process. During the next few days I prayed to God and the
angels to keep me safe. I asked God why, and though I
knew I was being given an answer, the noise in my head
overpowered it.

This experience changed me forever. I walked into the facility a rebellious teenager, and walked out broken and not
trusting anyone, including my family. My heart was not the
same towards people, particularly my father, the man I'd
once trusted more than anyone in the world. He had failed
me and lied to me.

I expressed how shattered I felt in poems I would write in
solitude to heal myself and release my pains, hurts, frustra-
tions, and change of heart. And still I smiled.

The rest of high school flew by. I had different friends, ran
track, had my share of boyfriends, and was mentored by
two special teachers who gave me hope in people again.
One was Mr. Vargas, a biology teacher. A free-spirited man
who always smiled, he loved the ocean even more than I
did. The man wore a permanent smile, as I did. The only
difference between our smiles was that his came from a
real inner happiness, radiating outwardly. Mine was there to
keep the game face of happiness visible, while a piece of
me inside had died.

I went to Mr. Vargas's class not so much eager to learn as
eager to hear him speak positively about things and see the
beauty of his smile and the light in his eyes. That daily rou-

tine cracked some light into my closed and darkened heart, which very slowly began to open again to let light in.

Miss Rains was my very favorite teacher and the only one I kept in contact with after I graduated. She taught the arts, which I took for two years. This human angel was a rarity in the school system. She was loving and compassionate, and though she'd been involved in theater and teaching for many years she still loved what she taught. Her very being radiated her love of acting and the theater. This special lady was heaven-sent to be a mother. She had adopted seven or more children from different nationalities. Those kids had a wonderful goddess of a mother. Throughout the years, the children would visit her in class. If ever there was a family that epitomized love, adoration, and respect, it would be Miss Rains' family, even though she was a single mom and all of her kids were grown.

Miss Rains was abundant in many respects. Incredibly obese, she used a cane to walk. She had a smile and laugh that could be felt across the campus and a heart as pure and giving as the saints themselves. She knew how to bring out the best in all students, especially me. She helped me build confidence in myself and my abilities, a foundation that I'd lacked to that point. She was my biggest cheerleader, teacher, and a human angel who opened my mind to my own greatness. She taught me to use fear as a tool to get where I needed to go, and not as a crutch.

Miss Rains was the teacher who taught me to believe in myself and the importance of having a golden heart in every situation. For this, I will be forever grateful. It is her words that echo in my head whenever I feel like giving up. This was my first human angel encounter, and fortunately, instead of disappearing when our class ended, she remained a prominent part of my life throughout high school. Even when I did not have her on my roster, I visited her class to say hello and chat instead of going to the cafeteria at lunch. After all, I called her "Mom" at school, and she treated me as if I was her own.

Those were two of my favorite teachers: one a male hippie and one a female cherub. Let me introduce you now to the one I called the Enforcer. She was my track coach at the high school and her name was Misses P. A Spanish beauty with short, curly hair, a banging body, and an "I'm here to win with no exceptions" attitude, this woman had the emotions, strength, and demeanor of a bull. She had an eye for talent and was serious about her sport.

Misses P pushed me harder than anyone ever did in my life. I thought she could be cool at times, but I also disliked her. Why? Because I felt she played favorites and was always getting on my case to do better, push harder, do it again until it was right. The way she spoke to me was different than the other students. She spoke to the other girls on the varsity track team as if they were her friends. When she addressed me, I got toughness from her—not anger, but serious sternness.

One day after school, we had a track practice where I felt I was being picked on. After a while I'd enough. I walked off the field. The coach followed. We stopped in front of the gymnasium steps, where, with tears coming down my face,

I asked her why she hated me so much, why she always picked on me. She told me she saw greatness in me and knew I could do better than what I was giving. She saw a leader who needed molding through tough love.

Misses P went on to explain how she liked me and needed me to give the 100 percent in practices that I already gave on meet days. My point of view on her and on the way others had treated me in the past from that point onward molded into one big lesson of them believing in me more than I had believed in myself. It showed me their willingness to push greatness out of me even if I kicked and screamed the entire way.

CHAPTER 3

GROWTH THROUGH LOSS AND BIRTH

I attended college away from home for a couple of years before realizing it was not for me. During this brief time, I became pregnant, got my first tattoo, and one of the most important men in my life passed away. The birth and death in my life triggered a spiritual rebirth within me.

Freshman year, some of my girlfriends and I decided to get tattoos. Mine was my name, placed on my thigh. It was not my full name, but my nickname: the name that only family or those close to me would call me. I chose it as the first of, at present, twenty-two tattoos on my body because of the importance of knowing who I am, where I came from, and what my inner child will always be known as. I do not regret that first tattoo and when I catch glimpses of it, I am always reminded of the first chapters of my life.

During the summer of my first year in college, I got pregnant with my daughter, Light, and moved in with my parents for the pregnancy and part of her first year of life. Initially, one parent told me I should get an abortion and the other supported my decision, whatever I chose. Both knew I had no plans on staying with the father of my child. Perhaps one or both felt it would be embarrassed having an unwed mother for a daughter. I'm not sure why they advised me as they did. The final decision was mine, of course, and I chose to keep her.

I returned to college shortly after having Light, and a few months later I got a call that my Papa was in the hospital. My grandfather, whom I called Papa, had recovered from a stroke once before, so I assumed he'd recover again. My assumption was wrong. I got a second call telling me he didn't make it and my heart dropped to the ground. In my sorrow, I couldn't eat, let alone take care of a child on my own. I couldn't even bear to attend his funeral because of my deep pain. I wanted to mourn alone, and this I did with help from a few angelic friends: God and my paternal grandmother, Dorothy, who had passed in earlier years. The death of my grandfather took me pretty hard. I yelled at God for taking him away and feeling guilty for not showing up to his funeral. I was forced to question life: the real whos, whys, and whats versus what people are normally taught to believe. This began my journey of reawakening.

I moved back to live near my parents in South Texas. I lived in my own apartment and began reading avidly. I wanted to know more about God, but not from a religious point of view as I felt religions had too many rules. Inside, I did not feel that God could be as harsh as the Catholics say. I read books about Wicca, which allowed me to connect with nature, a connection I'd lost in my later teen years. In my early twenties, I would go out in nature and just be. I'd hug the trees and talk with the birds. I was able to feel my connection to every plant and animal. I loved and needed this connection.

I continued reading spiritual books and asking the angels to guide me to what I needed to learn. I picked up all sorts of books that taught me how to open my intuition, to help lost souls while I slept, to project myself astrally to different places and parts of the world, to see auras with my physical eyes (which quickly frightened me so I chose to close off the ability), to see the so-called unseen, and so much more. With my tiny baby by my side, I was in hermit stage being guided by so many wonderful assistants such as angels, passed relatives, Native Americans, as well as other controversial beings.

I was walking on new ground: scared, but eager and open. I had to place boundaries on what I was willing to see and in what form. The first time I had an encounter with a passed soul, it was my grandmother Dorothy, known as Dotty. I was lying in bed at my parents' house and felt someone rubbing one of my eyebrows, awakening me from my sleep. However, when I opened my eyes I saw no one. I closed my eyes and yet again someone's finger was rubbing my eyebrow. This time I also felt a warm sensation on my thigh and smelled a faint scent somewhat like the patchouli or frankincense that I often burned. In my head, I heard, "Relax your vision." This message was something I remembered reading in one of my many books. I opened my eyes and to my utter surprise I saw a huge white light with sparkling lights around it. I wasn't scared, but I had so much adrenaline running through my blood that I ran to go tell my dad.

Dad was watching TV late that night, sitting on the couch. His mother's energy was sparkling right next to him. I told my dad that his mother was right beside him. I don't think he believed me then, but it didn't matter. I was seeing what he couldn't and was grateful I could. I continued to tell him the story of how Dotty had gently awoken me from my sleep by rubbing my eyebrow. All of the sudden, the look in his eye changed. He gave me no verbal confirmation, but something inside me told me she used to rub his eyebrow as a child. The look I saw in his eyes said it all.

After a subsequent and frightening visit from my child's father's father, who was deceased, in my apartment one night, I laid down strict guidelines for my spiritual progression. I didn't want to see deceased people, other than my family members—and certainly not in a physical form. Rather, I was willing to see them as light energy, which did not frighten me. And so it was. I started seeing lights in different color and sizes depending on what and who spirits were that visited. From this point on, this has been how I am shown most angels, deceased spirits, elementals, and so on.

As I began to open up to a whole new world, my entire life shifted and I felt more aligned. I realized more was possible, and that as a child I was right to question spiritual teachings that did not resonate with me. I questioned not because I was being difficult, but because it did not sound like, or feel like, the truth.

That was when I began understanding the importance of a smile and what it was capable of. This was my means to begin the chapter of healing others in my way, with my uniqueness, and bless in a way that I knew would be illuminated by God's light.

CHAPTER 4

REBIRTH AND MY SPIRITUAL RENEWAL

When Light was two, I moved to Houston and began working at a well-known gym chain. I sat behind the front desk, smiling, greeting people, and laughing. The job was a perfect fit for me. I could make someone's day by smiling or paying them a sincere compliment. It felt amazing to spread positive energy. I worked at the gym for a couple of years and was so rewarded in spirit that I had extra energy to expel. This began my time and passion for working out.

From this point on, my physique, training, and proper eating regimen became very important to me. I cared how I looked. I didn't want to be someone who worked at a gym and did not look the part. I started exercising three days a week. My workouts mostly consisted of cardiovascular work and some light weight lifting. I trained to tone the body. I also gym hopped, and still do today. I loved the motivation I gained by moving from one environment to another. It was very inspiring. My competition was with my twin brother, which was more fun than anything else. We have similar genetics, and were always comparing our progress. His abs beat mine every time. His stomach was brick on brick, layered to perfection, whereas mine was a tapered V and would only ever show four distinct muscles. I loved the thickness of my hamstrings and quads, and worked hard to meet or beat the amazing, full calves he had.

While at the gym I met a beautiful girl. She was in the best shape I've ever seen a woman in. She became my motivation. Let me start by saying that although we did have a big Texas smile in common Holly was the total opposite of me physically. She was a tall, fair-skinned blond with blue eyes and I'm short and dark-skinned with dark hair and eyes. We would sometimes do cardio side by side and then go eat together right after. While she and I were not particularly close friends, we did like to discuss our life stories. I was impressed when she told me what she did for a living: modeling and exotic dancing.

I looked at her body and looked at mine and realized, "If Holly can model, so can I. My shape is just as amazing as hers." After that, I started doing local pictures and worked as an exotic dancer for a year, leaving the gym scene behind. At first, the lifestyle looked fun and was supposed to bring in great money. But as I worked, I realized it was not as glamorous as I had thought. I met all kinds of people, from politicians to average Joes. I had a couple of female acquaintances I enjoyed being around after work, but mostly I would work my shift at work and get back home to my daughter.

One day a new girl arrived at my job. She was soft spoken and chatted little the first day, but she said enough to inform me that she was intuitive. I thought this was amazing, since until then I had kept quiet about my gifts, not sharing them with anyone. Of all the places to meet another person who was conscious and proud of her abilities!

A few days later she came to work crying. I sat down with her to see what was going on, and she explained. Only then did I realize how many people felt comfortable confiding their troubles in me. Though I usually didn't give advice, I would listen. People usually left our conversations happier than they were when we first started talking. But let us get back to the crying beauty. She told me how abusive she had been with her body in many ways, including heavy drinking, unsafe sex, and illegal drug use. She handed me something: a beautiful quartz crystal.

I knew nothing about crystals and had never seen such a thing before. This was my first encounter. The crystal was pointed on one side and when I touched it, it gave me sharp pains in my head. A little fearfully, I graciously asked her why she was giving it to me. She explained how her guides told her to give it to me, as her own gifts would be closing down due to her lifestyle choices. I looked at her as though she was speaking like a person who had too many drinks. But somehow, looking into her eyes, I knew she was speaking the truth.

That experience left me with a number of realizations. One, I was healing my environment by listening—and yes, by smiling. Two, from the moment I looked into her eyes and for the rest of my life I knew I would be able to see, feel, and know the truth while people spoke to me. In my earlier years of opening to my spiritual gifts, I would either call someone out for their lack of truth or couldn't bear to look them in the eyes while they spoke falsely. It would hurt me to know that what they were speaking was not truth. Today, I observe and do not take it personally, as someone else's lie has nothing to do with me, but with their inner issues.

Lastly, I now possessed a beautiful crystal that caused me pain when I touched it. It would sit among my things for the next seven years before I cleared it by passing it along as a gift to someone else.

CHAPTER 5
A CAREER REBORN

I was ready to do great things. I was in great shape, remarkably healthy, had a little cutie (Light) on my hip. Ready for change, I would run in the early mornings and do focused meditations on what I desired in all parts of my life. This daily focusing while jogging produced great results. Among them, I met someone in Orlando, Florida, who opened the door for me to love and career success all in one.

I packed up my belongings and my tiny princess, and off to Florida we went. It was so amazing to have a fresh start and new experiences to enjoy. There was a gym right across the street from the apartment I lived in, sunshine almost every day, and the beach was only a short drive away. Not to mention I had a great guy at the time, Oliver, who would become the father of my other three princesses. I enjoyed everything about this place. I was a social butterfly in gyms and quickly met a couple of friends. And my fitness modeling career began in earnest.

Motivated by the new area and the beautiful physiques I saw there, I increased my fitness training sessions to five days a week. I paid even more attention to the food I ate and how it affected my body. I learned how to tweak my physique, transforming it from soft and toned to more muscular and defined using my food intake, exercise, and visualizations. It was amazing! At this point I was lifting more weights than ever and fully training every individual body part. My results were nothing short of my personal idea of my body's perfection. I was enjoying the fruits of my hard labor!

After a year in Orlando, I spoke with the owner of Nutrex, who happened to be my sweetheart at the time, about being used for their ads and joining the corporate team with all my southern hospitality and uniqueness. Before I knew it, I was being featured in ads for the company. From this point on, my life path was fitness. I pursued fitness by means of research and gaining personal insight on new ways to perfect the body. Each of our bodies can be individually perfected based on our goals and incorporating monumental lifestyle changes. I loved my body and felt at ease with maintaining or losing weight, adding muscle or softening parts. My ease with physical transformation in large is due to self-love and appreciation of my body. Now I had knowledge to share while living my dream of being a fitness model.

The Nutrex company was young, about three years old, and this was perfect for me. I truly loved their bodybuilding and fat-burning products, and their vitamins, and was impressed with their innovation when it came to delivering high-quality products. Nutrex is a trendsetter. The company was one of the first to offer liquid caps for fat burners, enabling their quick release in the body. By being in the ads for Nutrex, I was able to get my next break at Oxygen magazine by means of the publisher, the late Robert Kennedy, whom I called Bobby. He gave me my first layout. I was a very grateful girl for this new exposure and the Nutrex team I was with.

My first full feature in *Oxygen* was also made possible by Bobby. I adored, admired, and respected him wholeheartedly. He and his staff put me on the cover in 2010, and Bobby became my mentor and father figure in the industry before passing away in 2013. My experience of Bobby was that he was frank. He told me what needed to be worked on with my physique without holding back. He did not pay attention to the color of my skin, only the aesthetics of my female body. In the fitness industry, there is a lot of playing favorites and politics that go on, which are often served on a plate of broken promises. Bobby was not oblivious to the problems.

In a day and age where it is still rare to see women of color on magazine covers, Bobby worked to get me there. Publishers were still under the illusion that a black model would not sell their magazine to a Caucasian readership. Bobby ignored that. He was very fair and had a great eye for talent. He aimed for universality with the look of his covers. I admired that. To me, he was a living legend with fairness in his heart and a soft, authoritative wisdom his eyes. He has helped inspire me to live all of my dreams and remain authentic to myself. In part, he is why I am creating this autobiography, as well as pursuing other endeavors.

The last conversation I had with Bobby was upon arriving in Canada for a photo shoot. We had lunch and he told me, as he had so many times before, of my marketability with both glamour looks and fitness looks. He reminded me of how hesitant the staff had been when I first came on board with *Oxygen*. I told him I would be grateful forever for all he had done for me, for his honest pushing and mentoring. We changed the subject to him telling me how his company, Robert Kennedy Publishing, was doing as a whole at the time and about some of the losses he'd had in his life. He shared with me that he was writing a book about his different life experiences. I was excited to hear his story about how his life view had been shaped.

On that visit, I did a photo shoot. He briefly showed up at the end and told me he was pleased with my shape though he suggested I work to further sculpt my thighs. I gave him the last hug I would ever give him and said goodbye. Later, I mourned when I heard he had died. He was a great man who wanted to do great things and propelled many others to greatness. He was a living legend, a one-in–a-million type of person with a rare spirit. His work left a mark on my heart. The way he viewed and lived life imprinted on my soul.

While doing print work as a model, I continued my sponsorship with Nutrex. I also wrote two books and had three more daughters. After I was no longer in a relationship with my children's father, I felt ready for change in my career. I signed a nonexclusive contract with Sunwarrior, a vegan nutrition supplementation company, and moved away from the company, Nutrex, whose brand had helped start my fitness modeling career.

I fell in love with the owners of Sunwarrior and their organic products. These men knew more than an encyclopedia when it came to organics and how the human body assimilates plant material. I am still an ambassador for Sunwarrior and a cheerleader for the good they create in this world. They are a consciously aware group. Soon after I started working with Sunwarrior, I had a run of back-to-back magazine cover appearances. There were a couple of months where I landed covers for two different magazines. One was an online spiritual publication and the other a black fitness magazine. In 2013, I had more exposure in magazines than I'd ever had. I felt a level of success and achievement by this.

I love everything I do and do it sincerely. After seven years, I finally felt internally rewarded for my approach to fitness and spirituality. The two sides of me came together. I decided I would continue to do whatever I do with a message and a bang. My goals changed due to my internal victory. I became determined to write, speak, and spread the message to women to connect body, mind, and soul, and embrace a green lifestyle nutritionally and in their fashion choices. I will keep the specifics of how I plan to accomplish these objectives quiet for now. When they manifest, it will be like watching a beautiful blossom of flowers during the spring.

CHAPTER 6

AWAKENINGS AND ENCOUNTERS

At the beginning of 2011, the universe knocked on my door. I began living in a beautiful house that sat on the lake and feeling expansive. At my fingertips I had the serenity that my heart needed and yearned for: a beautiful house filled with natural light, glass, nature, and the ocean.

Every day I took a walk out to the lake and breathed the lake air. I would meditate, write, and do yoga on the dock. By reconnecting with nature I started regaining the wholeness that I felt I had lost a bit after living through certain of my experiences.

At night and early in the morning I would go outside and stare at the stars. This made me feel undeniably connected to the cosmos and all that existed in it. It was a soothing feeling, like connecting with home base. It was in the space I accessed within myself that I was reminded I was alive for a reason. I had to get busy fulfilling my spiritual mission because time does not stop. The world was waiting for my touch of light.

Although my fitness career continued uninterrupted, socially I became a bit of a hermit. I read more and more. I learned and observed intuitive messages that came to me daily through conversations I would hear, music, happenings, and strangers with messages sent just for me. Angels in human form would appear and disappear in the blink of my eye once a connection was made or message given. I was sometimes tested by the angels.

Everything is not what it appears to be, so we must not judge the miraculous in situations that appear petty or poverty stricken. I got to the point where I could feel the immanent presence without looking; I knew the angels were in the vicinity and would connect. They still pop up today when they feel the need, but mostly show themselves to me in their true form of light energy.

I was jolted one mind-awakening day when I bumped into a man while I was shopping at Barnes & Noble. I was waiting to be guided to the book I needed to read at the time. I often used to go to different bookstores to do this as my way of getting my books for class. It was like school for the spirit, being tested somehow on what I learned through any given encounter. While I cannot remember this particular man's name, I can remember feeling his presence before he approached me. I caught a hint of his position across the store before we got close. I have a distinct memory of his cane, his piercing eyes (like he saw what no one else could), and the black trench jacket he wore. As I scanned the books on the shelves, waiting for a title or image to pop out at me, I felt the man tuning in to my energy, which is how intuitives read people. I was uncomfortable with this, but calm. As I sat down on the bench behind him I spoke to him silently, telepathically asking him to refrain from reading my energy. He stopped scanning, but decided to have a seat next to me and share a message of what he had gathered intuitively off of me before I asked him to stop.

What the man described was me opening to a gift I believe I'll continue to use forever. He looked over at me and told me I would channel, that I was a conduit for messages that need to be shared through my words, either vocally or in writing. He saw the confusion in my eyes on hearing this. I knew that I did indeed have spiritual gifts, but channeling was not one of them. I felt quite perplexed and could only stare back. Before I was able to respond, he said something else. He quickly gave me a lesson on how to channel. He also asked me if I knew who Edgar Cayce was. I told him I did not know, but he told me he knew that I would go do my research. This stranger shared that there were more like me, that I was not alone. I smiled, said thank you, and walked away. I was a little shaken after leaving him, but would not forget that visit.

Something else happened while I was in the bookstore that day. As I mentioned earlier, angels sometimes appear to me in different places. That day was one of those days. Before the man's appearance and interaction, I walked passed a lady who had what I call a cherubic angel face. As I walked passed her, I felt the energy signature I recognize as an angel in human form. Something inside of me made me go on a moment before seeking this presence out.

While still on the same aisle as this fair-skinned, light-haired woman with a divine presence, I backtracked. One thing I learned early on about angels is how quickly they can disappear—literally. So I made eye contact with the woman and said hello. She smiled and I felt like the sun was gently penetrating my whole being. She also said a few more words I cannot remember. I knew the real message had not come from her mouth. I walked down to the end of the aisle and looked back to see if she was still there, and wasn't surprised to see her gone. I glanced around the store, which now felt empty. This encounter set the tone for the experience to follow. I knew something would happen. I just didn't know what.

CHAPTER 7

A LOVE OF CRYSTALS

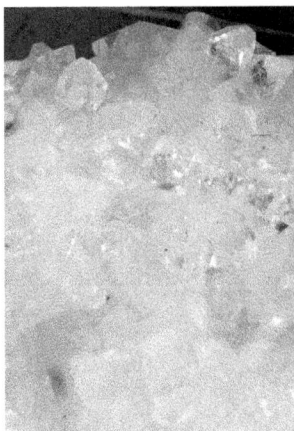

While staying at the big house on the lake, I reconnected with healing crystals. I do not know what triggered this connection, since I no longer had the crystal the exotic dancer gave me from some years back. I'd passed that on to a friend a couple years prior in whose possession it had been shattered. The first stones I felt drawn to purchase were a couple of basic crystals: a rose quartz, a smoky quartz, and a malachite. These were the ones I felt I needed.

In my studies I'd learned that crystals emit energy just like plants, animals, and human beings do. I was open to having a new experience—and why not? I had already learned much in my other dealings with unknown factors. I began adding to my collection of different beauties. I bought some crystals in their raw forms, and some crystal jewelry. These were placed in specific locations throughout the yard that felt appropriate.

I would often speak to a friend who was an intuitive and distance healer, and though she knew relatively little about them, she'd often be shown crystals that would be useful for me. I explained their properties to her and helped her understand what sort of crystal was good for what condition. There are hundreds of types of crystals in the world and I could not know everything about the crystals she was seeing because I had not read up on them. And yet I did know about them.

I found that I could tune in to a specific crystal with a thought of "getting to know it," and I would know what their benefits were, including information I had never seen printed. This ability drew me closer to the magical realm of fairies. Yes, I am one of those who believe in fairies; a belief that stems from my own direct experiences with them. The fairies, too, connect with crystals.

When I moved into the home where I live today, just outside of Orlando (and three miles away from a newly built church named Most Precious Blood), I planted my roots along with a whole array of crystals, even a crystal tree. Right from the start, this home made me feel even more expansive and safe than I felt before. For the first time in my life, my home was the source of my serenity, a place where I could be inspired to believe anything was possible. I was finally grounded enough to have a sincere love and gratitude for my space. I appreciate my land, the house I live in, the nature surrounding it, and all the animals that stop by to visit.

Once I felt in my own element my creativity exploded. I began writing a monthly meditation column for Bellésprit, an online magazine whose name in French means "beautiful spirit." My intent was to help others connect with the energies of crystals. I also wrote channelings from the archangels, since I had a close relationship with some of them. As I wrote, I connected with more and more higher beings. For the use of my crystal meditations, I only work with angels, channeling them, and the crystals. Bellésprit put me on the cover early in 2013 to showcase my gifts. I felt acknowledged in a much different way than I do in my fitness career.

Through fitness modeling, I was inspiring others with my physique and lifestyle. This is my passion. I was healing nature through my meditations, and healing those who read my column by awakening them to crystals and helping them to align, love, and let go. I was full in every public arena in which I was participating. I began getting increasing exposure, a couple times being featured simultaneously in different magazines. A few magazines hired me twice.

During the same period, I became able to channel more beings than angels. While working on my blog, I began channeling messages from a few ascended masters, God/Source, and other beings. I had harnessed my spiritual gift and now knew how to turn it on and off.

Crystals are a huge part of my identity. On a daily basis, I connect with their energy by wearing certain ones, sleeping with others, and of course, I have treasures buried on my property. They are my favorite gifts to receive. Most people who know me well will get one as a gift for me in some form.

One of nature's most precious gifts is to help us and adorn us with beautiful crystalline beings. Take a peek into any part of my world and it is crystals you will see.

CHAPTER 8

MY GIFTS

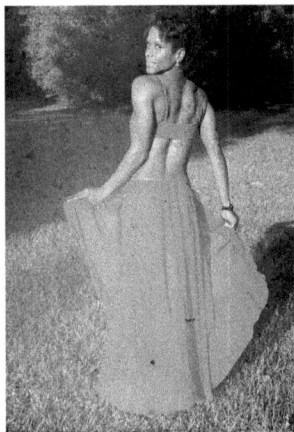

Just what are my spiritual gifts at this point? I have a few as I am a human channel, which allows me access to many methods to heal, teach, and share information. Below are some of my abilities. While these are the gifts I have opened up to now, I am confident I will continue to discover and develop more gifts during my lifetime. Before I explain them, understand that everyone has abilities of some kind. Some come naturally. Others take practice.

Healing. I allow energy to flow through me in order to heal nature and people.

Sight. I am able to see energies that usually are invisible to the naked eye. These energies are communities of beings. I see them as energy balls, or orbs, which vary in size depending on who or what they are. These are a bit like the stars at night. I can see energy on people as they heal and when they get mad. I do not see an aura on anyone except myself, but my aura lets me know what energy is flowing through it based on colors I see. I see other people's energy as specks of light, arriving in singles or in groups like a firecracker.

Truth in the eyes. I am able to see truth in a person standing directly in front of me. I can look in their eyes and ask for truth. The eyes cannot show anything but truth. So as a person speaks, what is transmitted to my mind would either be the truth or a muffled quality. I seem not allowed to hear what actually comes out of a person's mouth unless it is truthful.

Channeling. While there are a couple different ways possible to channel, I channel consciously. I connect with angels, fairies, spirits that have passed on, and more. I allow them to communicate with me through images, words, and feelings.

Claircognizance. This is a knowing. I can ask questions and instead of hearing answers, I know them automatically. It is a strong, clear knowing. The answer pops up in my mind as a thought sometimes before I even finish the question. This happens before the ego-mind can interject and rationalize its opinion.

Automatic writing. Here I allow a message to flow directly through my hands, with no interference from my mind.

Empathy. I can feel another person's emotions, pains, and more. While empathy is a great gift, it makes me sensitive to the people who come around.

Faith healing and energy healing. When I employ these gifts, it is in combination. Faith healing is the power of believing that a person or a situation is able to heal. Energy healing is where I am letting energy flow from my hands while placed on another. I do something similar when I am trying to do earth healing and nature healings. I allow the energy of my entire body to open as a vessel to transmit energy.

I learn about new abilities every day. Of them all, the biggest gift is being open and receptive without judgment.

CHAPTER 9

MOTHERHOOD

In the mixture of all this me is a whole lot of *shes.*

My daughter Light, the eldest of my four girls, has a good heart and mind. Much like her mother, she goes through her painful emotions silently and in solitude. She was my first child, born when I was young. Light was the only one of my children that I ever spanked as a form of discipline, and fortunately I only did so for a short time. Through the experience I realized that I wasn't teaching her to do right by spanking her. I was teaching her to fear me, not respect me. Through the transition of my awakening in Texas, I stopped using force and began to use an alternative approach to discipline that worked much better. By the end, I was guiding her with love instead of pain. She will lead one day with love and fairness because that is who she is.

My second pregnancy was rough. At the time, I wasn't in the happiest of places in my relationship with Tatjana's father and so I felt somewhat isolated. My emotions and the toxicity of the situation manifested as two painful cysts lodged in my reproductive system. They both started off small, but as my child grew inside of me, so did they. I had them removed shortly after Tatjana's birth, as their presence was very uncomfortable. One was the size of a grapefruit and the other the size of a lemon. Luckily, the cysts were benign.

Tatjana had a distinctive personality from the beginning. She was ready to take over the world and do it all now. She is a gentle-hearted diva, shy, but once able to master something will show it off often. She has an imagination to manifest the world, and can wonder for days. A lot like her mama, she loves singing, fairies, and crystals.

My third and final pregnancy brought me beautiful twin princesses. This was another emotionally difficult pregnancy for me and also the toughest on my body. The experience was awe inspiring, and gave me new admiration for the female body: not only its ability to grow life, but also its resilience. My goal for my third pregnancy was to eat the same as I did with each of my earlier pregnancies, and get my normally toned body to warp into the shape of the average American women who was pregnant or a little overweight. This was done not to give me a physical advantage over the average women, but to enable these women, from their current starting points, to get the weight gone without many of the excuses.

I was with the man I loved, but felt unsupported, just as I had during my second pregnancy, although this time for other reasons. A month before the birth, I made the decision to be a single mother. My beautiful twins came early due to my stress, but were kicking and screaming and healthy when they came out. They lived in the hospital for the first couple of weeks of their lives, just like their mother.

Sophia is the elder of the two twins. She is independent and loves nature and is a tomboy. The most athletic of my girls she is the one who most closely resembles me. Free spirited, she follows the beat of her own drum with intermissions from her twin sister, Olivia.

Now, Olivia is the diva of my girls—though she and Tatjana run a tight race for this distinction. Very dramatic, vocal, and loud, she loves attention. Olivia is a thinker, doer, and achiever. She analyzes situations, is smart, and has an excellent memory. She has a face of an angel and the temperament of a diva.

All of my girls mirror sides of me, including sides that I sometimes forget I have. I am constantly learning from these girls and they are my source of unconditional love. Together we live in a household full of spiciness, sparkles, lip gloss, and dirt, and unconditional love. I wouldn't have it any other way.

PART TWO

TRANSFORM YOUR WORLD— SELF-HELP

CHAPTER 10

THE FORMULA

Being a fitness model, keeping my body's image was important during my last pregnancy. It was important to me not to put on more than the average weight a woman pregnant with twins does and then to lose the baby weight in record time. Fitness model or not, I am confident that a weight loss of over fifty pounds is obtainable with dedication, hard work, and devotion to yourself. Once you know the tools, there is no real excuse not to loss weight if you give it your all, stay motivated, and dedicate yourself to the weight loss. That's how I succeeded.

With me being thirty-three, and this being my third pregnancy, we cannot dismiss the melting off of the fifty pounds I'd gained as being due to a fast metabolism. The only source of my accomplishment was my love of my body, hard work, motivation, and the dedication I put into weight loss. I had to put in the work, I had to monitor what went in my belly, and I had to find the motivation and dedication needed to accomplish this objective.

Even after having birthed four beautiful girls, I am in the best shape of my life. I have watched and felt my body put on weight ranging up to sixty pounds over my pre-pregnancy weight. While I was pregnant I was a butterball and I loved it! When I tell people how much I gained in all these pregnancies, their jaws usually drop. This is because most people cannot tell now that I was ever pregnant unless they see me with my beautiful girls.

How did I gain so much weight during pregnancy? I ate foods outside my normal diet. I kept my body nourished with what it needed and more, but also made it a point to over indulge, even eating fast food and junk food a few days a week. While I do not recommend this eating behavior for you new mommies to be, I was never in danger, nor did I endanger my babies. From previous pregnancies and also from the way I have learned to transform my physique from soft and toned to tight and lean for pictures, I knew my body's capabilities.

Many people have asked me why I would allow my body weight to fluctuate so much. It is simple: I did it to prove a point. I wanted to prove a point to moms who use pregnancy to justify why they let go of their bodies and stop caring. Three times over I've removed this excuse for weight gain and poor fitness, making this rationalization irrelevant by being proof of the opposite. I was able to use my pregnancy as a motivation to show how resilient the body is and what it is capable of doing with hard work and self-love.

The next reason I decided purposefully to undergo a huge weight gain is as a demonstration for young couples. Often people are frightened of having children because they feel they have so little time for themselves or their bodies already. I wanted to show them that it is possible to get pregnant one, two, and even three times and still get your pre-pregnancy body back by choosing to do so and following through. You are the master of your body. I also wanted moms and dads with young children to know that fitness can remain a part of their lives.

The best part of my weight-loss formula was that it would not fail. The formula stayed the same throughout each of my weight-loss periods. With a couple of tweaks, the original formula I invented works for me in losing and maintaining the weight without rebounds.

So what is this formula? What is this all about and why has it worked for me without fail after each pregnancy? And how do I know that it is possible for this formula to work for you, too? These are some of the questions I will answer for you in this chapter. I have four beautiful children and I have undoubtedly managed my weight for over seventeen years. The results speak for themselves. I am living proof.

When you are ready to take control of your life and make a lifelong lifestyle change, read on.

THE FORMULA

1. Incorporating a healthy lifestyle and ridding the mental program of diets.

2. Visualizing.

3. Believe in you.

4. Putting in the work.

5. Loving you.

INCORPORATING A HEALTHY LIFESTYLE

The formula starts with you making a choice about the direction of your life. This choice is yours, and yours alone, to make. You have to acknowledge the lack of success you've had in the past, as it pertains to your body, if you have tried and failed to make change before. This includes, but is not limited to, clearly admitting to yourself such things as not devoting 100 percent of yourself towards achieving and maintaining your weight goals, not making enough time to take care of yourself, wanting a magic pill to somehow do the work for you, and most importantly, not feeling enough self-love.

You must begin then by making a promise that you will start treating yourself, and that body of yours, better. Remember that this choice has to be made solely for you. You can only succeed in the long run by doing this for yourself and not for others or because of what they think of you. The fact of the matter is that it is about you wanting to lead a healthy, happy life, which stems from your own desires or needs. The future of your physical success is in your hands. You must decide to do this, and then lovingly follow through. Know that every success requires hard work and perseverance. Every day you will be presented with challenges giving you an opportunity to prove just how strong and magnificent you are.

It is in you. You just need to make the choice to succeed.

Chances are, up until today, you gave your power away. What does this have to do with weight? Everything. When we take control of our lives, we are empowered. If, on the other hand, you allow food, people, and circumstances to be your crutches in life, or to sabotage your success, you have given these objects power over you. Think for a moment. Where are you today, physically speaking, and why? What traps have you allowed yourself to fall in? How has food been your comfort? How has weight been your crutch?

I am going to give you my own personal reasons of how I have used food as comfort and weight as a crutch. Food is, hands down the quickest form of comfort in times of emotional situations and traumas. When I was sad, upset, and stressed out, food was the first outlet I took. It is easily available at all times, so why not?

The added pounds of fat are why not! I now know that there are healthier outlets for my upset, such as exercise, meditation, and writing. These are methods I use today and have enabled me to take back the personal power that I once gave to food.

As far as weight being used as a crutch, what I have noticed in my personal life is that less has been expected of me when I was heavier. Thus, when I was heavier I had less pressure to perform based on outer expectations and less need to maintain a certain image based on outer approval. Image-driven people communicate less with those who are not, and at times I needed to be in that quiet place.

What I have noticed in my life in dealing with my personal image and weight is that when my physique is changed, be that to a softer, toned image, or to a more muscular (though still feminine) image, either way the result has stemmed from my motivation. What prompted me to choose a softer look or more defined look? Was it my own expectation and love of my abilities to change my physique as a chameleon does? Or was it based off of what others expected me to look like? The best results and best images shot of me were taken with me looking the way I felt I should look. Each photo shoot leaves me looking better and better because today

I am completely where I need to be: I accept myself and don't abide by the pressures of others.

Let go of the crutch. The choice is yours.

The scariest and least productive part of getting into shape is the "D" word. I am talking about the word *diet.* This word needs to be erased from your psyche. Look at the word for a moment. The first three letters spell die, and rightfully so, as most diets cause more harm to the body than good. Diets fit nowhere in a healthy lifestyle and will only instill you with the idea that you are not enough. What you do through dieting does not show love to your body or your spirit. You were born in God's perfect image. Remember this.

While we can always make improvements, the changes we make must incorporate love. How is this done? A lot of it comes down to what you feed your "vehicle." Starving yourself does not work on any level: not emotionally, physically, or spiritually. Your body needs nourishment, to eat certain foods not because you are told to, but because you love your body and want it to look and feel its best. Love causes you to feed it the best nourishment.

I am not saying to never again eat sugar, high salts, or junk food. What I am saying is, eat it as a reward once or twice a week. Even right before and after a shoot, I reward my body for performing well and giving me the results I needed for the images. Then I indulge in a sweet treat of my choosing. A good lifestyle allows for a balance composed mainly of what we consider healthy foods and a sprinkle of those we consider not so healthy.

In my everyday life, I eat pretty well, and I also allow rewards a few times a week. It is usually two weeks prior to an event or shoot that I pay particular attention to what I put inside of my body. I have to nourish my body with the foods that will be optimal for achieving the look I am trying to achieve. Notice that I said "two weeks prior." When you're leading a healthy lifestyle, you do not rebound to higher weight following a weight loss. What a beautiful thing this is. Because my weight doesn't fluctuate much, you won't catch me more than three to five pounds over or under the weight I like to sit at.

I love my body and know what it is capable of.

VISUALIZATION

Visualization was, is, and will always be important for me in terms of both weight loss and weight maintenance. I feel we have to be able to see the goal in our minds. We have to know our goal is possible.

Chances are, if you can see your goal and hold that focus clearly, you already have a form of belief in yourself and your ability to get your body where it needs to be. I stress the importance of visualizing yourself to your perfection, rather than to someone else's.

I have said it before and will say it again: Your body is unique. Period. There will never be another you, just as there will never be another me. Love the skin you are in, and perfect it to its best. Got it? Good.

What is involved in visualizing? You must hold a picture in your mind. Close your eyes. Can you clearly see what was in front of you? Open your eyes and look at what is directly in front of you—something other than this book. As clearly as you see with your eyes open, that's how clearly you want to see with your eyes closed during visualization. This degree of clarity is possible and takes practice. This is how we will entrain the mind.

The image you want to see in the mirror of yourself should be seen first in your mind. You want and need to be able to see this as vividly as possible. Then imagine how you would feel if you were at this weight. Would you smile more? Would your attire be more neatly kept? If you can hold this image with the feeling of happiness and love long enough, it is bound to become your reality.

You might ask what benefit the process of visualizing has on weight loss? Good question. It programs the sometimes stubborn subconscious into manifesting in the physical. This ability entrains and retrains the mind, and your whole being, into believing your goal is possible. You're telling your brain that this is what you expect delivered to perfection. It is kind of like putting in an order at a restaurant. Your eyes scan down the menu, visualizing what the item might look and taste like. Once you have found what you desire, you order it and, of course, expect it to be hand delivered perfectly to your instructions. Your body-mind works the same way, like a waiter at your service that needs your guidance as to what you desire.

BELIEVING IN YOU

You will always be the reason behind your biggest successes or failures in anything. Weight loss and maintenance are no different.

The truth of the matter is that some days flow easier than others. The joy in leading a healthy lifestyle is that there is always a win-win situation: meaning, the days you feel you are struggling more or falling off your plan remind you to just take the journey day by day, moment by moment. Those steps, whether they require little effort or great striving, are steps needed for lasting results.

The body needs breaks from what we normally do to it and feed it. Similarly, the mind needs variety. Human beings need to be mentally stimulated, they feed off of variety. The body loves that stimulating change as well.

Remember that it is important to let go of what you've learned from the past about weight loss and weight management. Diets do not work in the long term and I do not condone them. Each body is unique to its owner, including the bodies of twins. The results you achieve come from the effort, work, and love you put into redefining your body and its image. Your body can only be perfected to its own capabilities and will never look like your neighbors' or friends' bodies or the bodies of people on the cover of magazines.

I have personally attempted to emulate someone else's body without satisfactory results. I used my twin brother's abs as my motivation. My brother had what I considered perfect abs. We were designed by the same parents, but even with us, nearly as genetically close as it comes, we were far apart in our build. In saying this, the bodies we admire have been perfected to their greatness, and should only be used as motivation for you to get focused and in gear.

Your belief is like a magical wand. You just focus and believe, and it is so. For those who have trouble trusting the process and believing that your dream body is possible, take one month to have the imagination of a child about it and openheartedly believe. What is the worst that could happen? You know you're not going to die from imagination.

The best that could happen is that you experience the power of your own mind, body, and spirit producing the results you are visualizing. I am not saying the transformation will happen overnight. I am telling you that, yes, it is very possible.

PUTTING IN THE WORK

You have to be willing to put in the work needed to achieve the physique you desire. Many people today expect a quick fix—overnight results. This is not a healthy mind frame, nor is it as gratifying as the journey of getting your body where it needs to be. There is a beauty in transforming your body with love. The mind and the heart transform as well. That is not a process worth skipping, as you don't want to miss out on the gratification of accomplishing something wonderful for yourself.

One hundred percent dedication earns you satisfaction guaranteed. No one else is going to put in the work to get your body in its best shape. We have gotten to a place where, throughout the generations, we have gotten lazier as opposed to more active and healthier. The United States is one of the fattest and laziest countries in the world. There was a time when our people loved being outdoors, running around in nature, playing, and exercising. These days our lifestyle is far more sedentary. Technology, rather than nature, rules our world.

I am not saying all people are this way, but many are. So many people are like this, in fact, that it has trickled down to the younger generation. They see what we as parents and adults consume and then think it is healthy. It is time to regain control of our bellies and lifestyles. Amp it up. It is a win-win for you and your family. It is a winning lifestyle.

When you go to the gym or do your workouts at home, do it with all you've got. This is a present for you, from you. You should be fully enveloped in the moment with each exercise, each set, each movement. If you are exercising for thirty minutes to an hour, understand that this is a tiny percentage of the twenty-four hours you have in every day. You owe it to yourself to be fully present as a part of your "me" time.

Putting forth half the effort will give, at most, half the result you want to see. The point is you will still fall short and then have no one to blame but yourself. You are held accountable for where you are in this journey. We do not like it when people half complete something we have asked them to do. Let us lead by example and show ourselves and those around us the reward that comes from completion in the feeling and look of what giving your all is capable of.

LOVING YOU

I will touch on self-love here as part of the formula, and again later in the book, as it is important in every aspect of your life. Let us start with the role self-love plays in weight loss and management. It is crucial, and my own experience has brought me to the conclusion that self-love is the most important ingredient found in the formula for long-lasting success.

You have to start from a solid foundation to have solid results. What better than the foundation of loving you? When we focus on the things we love and appreciate in our bodies, we continue to add more beauty to those areas. You align yourself with a frequency of love that comes from within. Your cells, muscles, skin, and other organs are affected by this. You open up to an invisible world of endless possibilities that you can manifest through yourself.

We can stare in the mirror and complain about the parts of ourselves we see as flawed. It will become our own downfall. Or we can choose to focus on the beauty that we possess, and accept that what we consider as flaws are anything but. We are all very beautiful. You have to see, know, feel, and believe you are beautiful. You must know that you are love in order for others to see it. The truth is that the part of yourself that you are complaining about, someone else is wishing they had. Be grateful for your body, and your body will show how grateful it is to you.

If for no other reason than that you are still here today, be grateful and loving to yourself. What we feel we lack, another lacks more. For that scar on your knee you complain of, think of how envious someone without legs would be of your unique wound. All I am saying is to put things into perspective here. You are damn beautiful, handsome! Take your power and own it. Know that your body is a gift and should be treated with love for loving results.

Loving yourself allows you to love others and show them how to love you. The more you truly love yourself the more those supportive, loving people will be drawn to you and enter your life. You are a beautiful message of love not despite your perceived faults, but because of them. You are and always will be love in each experience. You are love.

CHAPTER 11
SELF-LOVE

Let us delve more into self-love as it pertains to your entire life and the world around you. It is so vital that I need to thoroughly stress the importance of this love. How you love yourself has a rippling effect within your being, your environment, and the world as a whole.

One of our greatest desires is to love and be loved, and it all begins with you. Do you accept all of who you are? Do you appreciate all of the wonderful traits and characteristics that make you, you? Do you know how to love yourself utterly and completely? Many do not, and many more, me included, still have more accepting and self-loving to do.

The absence of what these two words, *self* and *love,* represent is at the root of every disharmony we can experience in relationships, causing disease within the body and conflict within the world. Many people lack self-love. I am not excluded from this assertion by any means. I love myself today more than I ever have and still I am learning to love myself completely. I would not change the life I have lived for anyone else's. I would not change one thing about my experiences, for I do not believe in regret. I would not change a thing about the many loves and pains I have experienced, and why should I? Those experiences brought me to the point of acceptance and self-love I experience today. They are how I learned to be much less judgmental than I ever was before.

How can we expect another person to know and love us the way we desire if we don't know how to love and fully accept ourselves? You could search the world a thousand times over for loving relationships and experiences to no avail. You are the vessel of love and it is from within you that love will manifest in your life. Until we learn to love ourselves there will always be a void left unfulfilled. Your heart is waiting, a golden door just for you to open, and enter its chambers of truth and deep love.

You see, I was always good at smiling publicly through pain and sadness because that is who I am. I could not hide from my hurts or sensitivities as they echoed in my mind and I felt their weight on my shoulders. I am supposed to be strong, for myself and many others, and I am expected not to show pain and emotions other than love. But the reality is that I do hurt at times from my experiences as much as anyone does. I want to go outside and scream and cry, and today I do so sometimes instead of holding my painful feelings in.

It took me losing my sense of self and listening to other people's opinions about me, my existence, my career, and who they thought I was to learn self-love. Now I know that my life is created by me and moves forward by my actions.

No one will ever know you better than you know yourself. Do not let the words of others matter. If they are spitting out toxicity, remove them from you experience. Let them go so that a higher, more loving experience can come in.

- When we do not love ourselves, we fear others.

- When we do not love ourselves, we hate another.

- When we do not love ourselves and hold on to negative emotions or experiences, the toxicity can manifest as illnesses and other physical ailments.

Living life does not mean we won't experience things that throw us off balance, or break us and shake our entire world. It is through those experiences that we learn that we are enough already. I love myself for my good heart and giving ways. I love myself with the physical scars left on the left side of my face, on my left knee, and the larger scar on my stomach. There is gratification in loving myself, although each day I choose to better myself in some way. I am me and love who I have become.

How would I know what pain was if I did not experience it in my own life? How would I understand yours? How could I know deep pains and hurts without feeling them myself? How could I let you know I have been where you have been, and remove myself from the pedestal you have placed me on because you thing I am better? If I didn't have traumas in my life, how could I feel so grateful for where I am today? I have hurt others and have been hurt. I have trusted people I shouldn't have trusted or believed in. There is a German saying that I love: *"So ist das Leben eben."* Such is life. I love myself through it all and I'm learning to love even more.

The truth is without my experiences, scars, and challenges, I would not be writing this book today. I would not understand the importance of love in each moment if I had never experienced it. And the same is as true of pain as it is of love. I have touched on my major challenges throughout this book, but what about the traumas that will never be written about? I had to go within, through divine guidance, so that I, too, could help you learn to love yourself without judgment, in order for you to fully love others without judgment.

What we feel and think about ourselves is reflected in the world outside of us. You can feel the inner joy and acceptance a person has when they walk by. This makes you feel a little lighter and more joyful. Your presence will affect the plants and animals that cross your path. This, in turn, will affect your whole day and everyone you interact with. When we learn to love ourselves, everything is okay and we realize that we're all connected. One person is not better than another; they only choose different experiences to regain their true essence of love.

Without love your world would be incomplete. By loving yourself, you love the world you live in. This world desperately needs the love which she has given all of us back in return. We are aiming for an equal giving and receiving flow, not just a taking and keeping. The plants and animals provide companionship, connections, and beautiful, loving scenery on your journey in life. It is time for us all to learn about a way to love that is true.

It is through self-love that we connect with the pure frequency of unconditional love. This love is so divine it has the power to heal any ailment, guaranteed. But if you cannot master and accept every part of yourself you deem unworthy, how are you to flow in harmony with a frequency that is much greater?

Karate is a perfect example of what I'm describing here. A person with a white belt is not on the same level as someone who has a black belt. And though one day he may earn that belt, it requires that he raise his skill level step by step with perseverance so that he too is able to match the energy and level of performance of someone with a black belt. We face the same type of situation when it comes to self-love. We must learn, through practice, how to love ourselves. Only then can we learn how to truly love another freely. Self-love will be our biggest challenge and we will have major experiences to bring us back to this unconditional love.

Your soul awaits your love, as does the whole world. Are you ready to master yourself?

THE GOOD IN IT ALL

What is my point for sharing these intimate parts of myself? I want you to know me for who I am and the path that has led me here. It is my wish that you understand the person behind the inspiration and how I came to be where I am. My spiritual mission was made known to me through my own experiences and solid connection to Source. It has not changed and will not change. In many ways I am here to help aid humanity and nature. I, too, will break my own barriers and master my own being through living, loving, and experiencing: This is what makes my heart flutter and fills my spirit.

I reveal my vulnerable moments to you in order to show that we share the same emotions and both of us have had painful experiences. I am also consciously aware of my gifts and my spiritual mission. That mission is first and foremost in my life. The quiet service I do will never cost anyone else a dime: It is my gift to the world. Along the way I have made some choices that are not the best. I have no regrets. This is how most of us learn life's lessons. I have an excellent ability to share messages from those who watch over us as written in my blogs and daily Facebook posts. And I have an equally important lust for life which is often taken for granted.

I am a vessel, as we are all vessels when we connect with the energy of creation. I am human and have pains and heartaches, as you do. My passion is fitness and modeling and this is how I get to live. It is my desire to inspire others into a healthy body and mind, and to help them let go of limits society has cast upon them. I do this through print, speech, training, working, and being. You see, in the beginning of my career, someone told me I was not going to get exposure in magazines outside of advertisements. I proved this naysayer wrong and I am still here, years later. Ironically, he has become one of the many people I work with on my magazine spreads.

I cannot be put in a box, though others may try to box me up. I have lived my life quietly, experiencing what I needed to in each moment to make me a better person and help me find the love in each situation. Though it is hard sometimes to see, the love story is there. Life is a love story where we are given opportunity after opportunity to expand our beliefs, to wash away false beliefs, and to come into our own.

We each have our own experiences and connections with God/Source. Find out what is true for you by experiencing it for yourself rather than listening to it out of the mouths of others. How can you truly understand if you do not experience, if you do not question? If you do not go within yourself, how can you understand what is outside of yourself? There were many questions I had and only one role model: my father. If you can find one person who is extraordinary, then observe this individual and ask him or her questions.

Never emulate another person. There is a beauty you deny both yourself and the world by not being authentically yourself. We are all beautiful creations with a story to tell. If you sit in silence or in judgment, you lose the connection of what is real. You and everything that exists in the world are love. You have always been love.

If something is not resonating with you in your own life, then by golly, recreate! You have the power to do so. I am not talking about an external discomfort, but something that does not feel right from the inside. Through my life I have learned the importance of love and questioning what does not resonate within my experience. I seek truth at its core from truth's direct source. I have realized that the attention and acceptance I seek is not from others, but from within. The world will unfold the way it is meant to in each moment. Losing precious time in worry and fear about the future, we forget to take notice of the moment. I have come to realize there are so many lost opportunities of love of good will, missed by not focusing on right now.

We all have our own life experiences, we have people who come and go, and we ourselves change. Our vibration raises and so does the quality of our experiences and interactions. We sometimes believe the worst: we feel like a victim and think we have such a horrible life. This is not the truth by any means. We are blessed to experience people and situations that help us to grow in each moment. This means that even if they are painful, they are not bad. They are great teachers if they have taught us to love, appreciate, and set boundaries for ourselves. We also teach others in our everyday interactions. We are given this opportunity to bring them back to the truth and love that resonates with them.

Yes, we will hurt others and get hurt in the process of living. We will lose people who are close to us, but then their spirits are reborn. I have learned that our loved ones are never really gone. We have access to them at all times through God/Source and the angelic realm. All we need to do is think of this person. It is as easy as that, and they are in our presence, if they were not already. Talk to them, and then listen. Answers are always given but we can only take notice if we are in the moment, awake, and open.

I have learned to be a lot less judgmental, though the goal is to be totally free of this mentality. It is not my duty to judge another, neither is it yours. People are where they are in life through their own choices, and although I may choose differently, it does not make me better than them. How hard it must be to come into this world and choose a path of love through the harshest experiences. Though we pass judgment on another, in the end that person will return to the full envelopment of unconditional love.

I have learned to quickly disengage myself from people and situations that do not resonate with me. This was learned through trial and error. I have a choice between going through the same patterns and creating authentic loving experiences surrounded by positive, empowering people. I came to this life so that I could heal others and myself through the movement of love divine.

I have opened up to and accepted my spiritual gifts, and in each moment I choose to use them in some loving way. The best I can do for you in this moment is to share some tools with you to help better yourself and the world. These words will awaken something in your heart. Be open to the messages in life, you have more power than you were taught, more power than some of you will ever know. It is all within and it always has been. Magic is found in the present. As you choose to live more in the present and choose more loving actions and thoughts, what you currently know as a miracle will become an everyday occurrence. Many who came before us have said we are capable of miracles. Stand in your power and freedom to heal, co-create, and be love. Start by cleaning up your world.

CHAPTER 12

GETTING STARTED: CLEAN UP YOUR WORLD

Cleaning up your world means clearing out the toxic people and moving away from the toxic places. Seek less anger and more love. Your body, your soul, and the outside world are affected by all that you do, whether or not you believe this. There are many people today who are consciously aware of this, but there are many more who still need to learn: to be made aware and open more fully to life and who they truly are. We are all connected. It took me a while to understand or believe this, but it is true. When our minds expand, so does our vision and true perception.

Life is all about love, so clean out the clutter in yours. Cleaning the clutter starts from within. I am not suggesting that you forget everything you have been taught about life.

What I am saying is to question what you were taught and be open to receiving new answers. When you live your life through those answers, your perception and experiences will change. You allow a more expansive experience and you are gifted with the truth. You will fill the truth into your entire being and it will feel like love and knowingness.

Make space in your being to let go of things you no longer need. This time more light and wisdom can be let in from the source of all. Clear your clutter and you clear clutters of the world around you. If you need proof, just ask. You are surrounded by beautiful, divine assistance that you may or may not be aware of.

If you are open to the answer, you will hear the answer.

If you are open to the answer, you will feel the answer.

If you are open to the answer, you will see the answer.

If you are open to the answer, you will know the answer.

The only limits that exist are the ones we have created. Shatter those walls and be receptive to all experiences, situations, and people and you will see the heart of the matter: You will see truth.

The choices you make create a domino effect, starting with your immediate environment and expanding into the rest of the world. If your energies shift, so do those around you, including those you may not think of as connected to you, like plants, rocks, animals, and so on. The truth is that you are a bundle of beautiful, magnificent energy, capable of 80 percent more than what you currently believe or were told. At the end of this life you will know this to be true. But if you are open to know it now, everything can shift. Your experiences and encounters will change in a way that shows you how great you truly are.

There have been many ascended masters, people such as Jesus, Quan Yin, Buddha, Lakshmi, and others throughout history who came to teach us. But because we put them on pedestals, we missed some of their message. You, too, can achieve your highest potential. You are your only limit and love is all that really exists when you see beneath the veil. Everything else is an illusion, the truth hidden from your eyes. If you do not agree, then at least question what I am suggesting. Experience the answer not through words that has been entrained through the many years. You will see truth that needs no explanation, which needs no entrainment. It is raw, pure, and right there in your face.

I challenge you to simply ask: Why? Ask this not of another, but using your own way of connection ask it of God/Source, angels, and whatever else you are awake to. My promise is this: You will be told, see, feel, or know the truth. Will you be receptive? Messages come through all forms: something you read, hear, smell, see, or overhear in a conversation of some stranger in the store can be a message. You might even get a direct answer through another to you. Will you be able to feel the love that goes along with real truth and the authority behind it?

Clean your home and recycle things you don't need. Give things you have not used and don't plan on using to charities if they are still functioning and throw them away if they are not. Make room for new things in your home.

If there is space, new things will enter your life. But if there is clutter nothing new can ever fit. By cleaning house, you raise the vibrations and clear the energy of yourself and your home. Your own space affects everyone else. Your family will start feeling expansive and want to get rid of old things themselves. You won't even have to ask. Your energy affects them. What you do, so will another.

After you have cleaned your space, clean the furniture. Make it spotless. You are ready for a new flow of energy and experiences of truth and you are making sure the path is a straight shot. Have a seat and give thanks for a moment for the release of old, worn-out beliefs and experiences in your life, then give thanks for what is already on its way to you. You can do it, you are greatness, and it is time to awaken to it.

Challenges and choices are character builders, tests to show us our own strength. What I have learned is that we repeat the lessons we do not learn. We ask: Why would a God/Source who loves us allow us to go through the pain of some of these challenges? Here is your answer: God/Source has unconditional love for us and knows we return to that place within us which is closest to God/Source during these challenges. He/She does not intervene in the choices we make in these challenges. He/She knows that if we are repeating a challenge it is because we are not yet ready to move away from that challenge to another. Free will allows this. My experience of God/Source is not a vengeful one, and the love is unconditional, without judgment. We as people bring the judgment and fear into the relationship.

I feel everything happens for a reason, exactly when it is supposed to, and we respond exactly as we are supposed to respond in that moment. While some challenges we fly past once, other challenges may take a couple more tries before we learn and understand the message being shown us.

We learn who we are as individuals, as a people, and as spirit through our choices and the challenges we face. It gives us the opportunity to see how strong and beautifully divine we each are. We are taught about love on all levels, leading us back to the largest and most unified love in the universe: unconditional love.

SOMETHING MAGICAL

When you blend belief of the impossible with unconditional love, endless opportunities flow into your life. There is something magical about belief and love. You see, it does not matter what someone believes is possible for you, it matters that you believe within yourself that anything is possible. It does not matter if someone believes your truth or not. Your truth needs no defending or explanation. I believe the two most important energies readily available to us to create and make miracles happen every day are the vibrations of belief and the vibration of love.

I am not talking about a love with limits and judgments, but the purest love at our fingertips seen daily in our world. Unconditional love is so pure and divine that its effect, its power, causes all else in its field to match it, to heal in its presence, to ascend to its higher vibration, and surrender to it. There will be a day when the first option in healing disease or pain is sending love, raising the vibration of a cell through the language of light. But that can happen only when the world is ready, when the world realizes who they are and their own great abilities.

As many of you know, my messages all end with love. Love combined with belief heals all things and situations. It makes the impossible possible for the one who believes in themselves. I was born and told I might not make it outside of the hospital walls. I was told I would never get magazine exposure due to skin color and my lack of competition credentials. I have had many false things said about me by others who believe I am something I am not.

I make miracles happen daily. What I believe my experiences in life make possible. If you ask anyone who has spent a couple of days on my property, they will tell you that mine is a house where magic happens. It is my belief, my openness, my love for everything that exists in this world that makes it so. Even after deep hurts and hard struggles, still I smile. I will always know the truth of what is possible, and offer to help you open up to new possibilities. Try it for a week and you will notice major change in yourself. You will see your world, your mind, and your possibilities shift and draw these wonderful experiences to you.

All I am asking of you, for you, is to believe with all your heart that there is more than what you currently know in life. Open to a surreal love and share it unconditionally with those around you. The world needs this. You need this. One thought changes everything, one action changes everything. Believe in yourself and love yourself enough to know that miracles can and do happen daily. You are one of those remarkable miracles. Remember that. You are here today after all you have been through, all you have lived through. It is time to make magic happen.

CHAPTER 13
CHANNELED MESSAGES

We are all one. The trees, the ocean, the sun, each of you. You are here to learn and grow as a whole. As one consciousness. There is a void right now that many of you are trying to fill. Yet you still feel empty. Why is this? You think that you are alone. You are not. Every action that you set into motion affects every person, place, and thing in your world. Some of you are aware of this while others choose not to accept that this is the reality.

You have a planet on which you live named Earth that is a masterpiece created by all of you and disintegrating because of all of you as a whole. Wake up. You will be in a state of emergency and need each other more than you think. Materialism will fall by the wayside. Energy. It is all a form of energy and you must ascend now. You will be reborn as a consciousness as a whole. Much like the waste you rid yourself of in the trash. The whole consciousness that you all are will do the same. It is by choice and free will that this has come to be.

There is a higher purpose than your everyday individual money, cars, boats, and so on. You are here to ascend in light, to transcend all into love, bringing all things back to their natural state: love. You have the power to create and co-create, yet you act as if you are powerless. You know all things, but act as if you are without knowledge. Beings of light, remember who you are. You are everything and know all. You are not powerless, as you have created both your current state, the status of yourself as an individual and your circumstances, as well as the destruction and denigration of the place you call home. Mother Earth.

Heal yourself. Feel yourself. You are grand and have much work to do in such little time. But it is possible. You all, in unison, need each other. Do not forget this, as this is what it took to create this place. This is the same energy of light and love you need to ascend this world as well as yourself. You are moving to a higher vibration and old parts of the whole that you are will die off until you are back to your natural state. A higher state and consciously aware of this.

Light, love, enlightenment, remembrance, evolution, and *ascension* are all key words that I encourage you to use as you embark on your inner journey back to a conscious oneness.

Love always,

—I am

Why is it important to go within?

There is nothing that exists that you do not already have knowledge of. But you must go within to get those answers. It sits inside of you, waiting for you to connect to your true being. There is nothing that exists that does not already exist inside of you first. You are a creator, here to create your outer world to look more like your inner world, your essence. You will remember who you are by sitting alone in silence. Anything and everything that exists and that will exist is created from a foundation of you.

Yes, you are an individual human being in life. Even greater is who you are as a whole. You are oneness consciousness, here to supersede the expectations of those before you, to grow and expand into the multidimensional being that you already exist as. This takes all of you, as a consciousness, choosing to allow this growth and path.

Haven't you realized you are much more than this body you are in? You have authentic power that is yours by right. Call upon this and use this to create a beautiful change. We are here to help and assist you now and have always been here through centuries. We love you.

—Oneness

Light workers

There are many of you light workers here now. And, those that are here to be the catalyst which bring about your light worker duties. While some of you will do this naturally, others will need to be lead from an inner push to do your light worker commitment. You all have a gift that will be used to help heal the oneness conscious. Embrace your gifts as you are divine and powerful beings. Your light will shine bright among those who need to heal. You will heal and be healed and raise the vibration of all.

While each of you have innate gifts, some will have more developed abilities in certain areas as this is what you have chosen. Your mission and message is of great importance and why you are surrounded by so many beings of love. You are protected always. Do not doubt your power, as you are powerful and create/manifest faster than those who are not light workers, but here to aid you here on this mission.

Stand tall, strong, and righteous in your movement on this earth as a light worker. We thank you and stand by your side as needed for guidance and protection.

—Oneness

Freedom/liberation

Freedom comes from within. Your answers, truth, guidance, knowledge, and remembrance come from here. You are a great being of light. A great beacon of light. You all look outside yourselves for the answers to you questions about love, peace, and God/Source. Source cannot exist without you as you are one in the same. Billions in this universe make up the oneness conscious God/Source.

You hurry in your everyday lives to get from point A to point B, do this and that. You lose yourself. There is a natural flow in life. It will continue to flow fluidly as you need only allow yourself to flow with it at its pace. Though you as people sometimes try, it cannot be broken or rushed to your satisfaction. That which happens in life happens as it should in the exact order and timing in which it should.

You are beautiful beings and need to spend time in a daily meditation to bring you back to who and what you are. Five to ten minutes is all you need. Just being in the present is a meditation. You need not be in any specific position or place other than the centered heart. Meditation is a reward to the soul, body, and mind and reconnects you to the whole that you are.

Your freedom and liberation come from within and not from any person or place which is outside of you. Go in.

—Oneness

Truth

Your actions must match your words. Truth is not only spoken in words, but shown through actions. You cannot have one without the other. It makes for falsehood. Many are scared to follow their inner truth. They have forgotten who they are and why they are here. You are all divine greatness. There is an inner truth and yearning waiting to spill out from the soul to you. Trust this feeling. Trust you.

May your words and actions be aligned in the great truth that you are, as a whole. One truth resonates with many seeking something more. Seeking the knowledge of the spiritual void they have. Truth is a yearning that is so great it is felt not only on a physical level, but your soul level as well. Truth's vibration is high as that of true love, divine love. Speak your truth and stand tall in it even if others doubt. Let them watch as everything you do is backed by the power of divine light and love. Either people will raise their vibration in truth or fall into nothingness.

Truth, light, love, are all that exist. Look for this inside of yourself. Here is where you will find it. You do not have to agree with the truth, yet search for it, acknowledge it, and accept this as so, and then and there you will know true victory.

—Oneness

Ask, then sit in silence

People always ask why their questions and prayers go un-answered. Let me explain, for there is not one single question that goes unanswered. The problem is in not listening. You must learn to sit still in silence. If you sit still only for a moment you will hear your answer. The mind is so cluttered with thoughts from before you asked your question and thoughts of what to do next in your day that you cannot hear in all that noise. So again we ask that you please learn to meditate and focus on nothing so that something can flow into your mind.

You are always answered immediately. The first attempt is at a thought, a feeling, a scent, and even knowingness. Sit in silence and hear the beauty of your soul's music play

—Oneness

Channeled From Galactic Being Lia

This light is what connects each and every one of you. One is not separate from the other though some may choose to experience life as they know it this way. The consciousness that calls you forth is that of divine light and love which you speak of. It is real and exists in the heart of the body and the light body of the soul. Everything is composed of this divinity. You either choose to experience the divine beauty in every situation or you don't. We are asking you all to choose a higher light, a higher way.

You are higher than the vibration that you are vibrating at and can choose to vibrate at a higher frequency at any time by asking and saying you are ready and we will help you vibrate at your highest capacity without causing your body harm. But with this comes you opening up your higher consciousness to a higher level. You must be willing and ready as this is not forced upon anyone. We love you and support your work, your mission, and you have our full blessing in your cause and that of all light workers who call on us to aid.

Light worker, diligently do your duty in love and light to the fullest as you are fully supported and whole. We love you all and await your full ascension.

Light and love,

Lia

Galactic Federation of Oneness

Oneness is accepting who you are as a whole. Your being exists because you willed it. Trust and know that all is okay, my child. These emotions you know as hurts will subside and you must learn to fully flow with them, through them. Everything that you are and will ever be you are composed of. Every piece of knowledge and information you will ever need you have full access to as it is your divine right, as is it to any other being.

The knowledge you and others need to heal your world is not hidden from you. It is already inside of you waiting like a book for you to open it and relearn. Remember as your ancestors before you have taught you. There is a reason for the demise of mankind of these years when it comes to knowledge. You have chosen to close it off. Acknowledge that the truth lies in every being with full access to it. Reclaim your knowledge stored in the back of your mind.

Healing can only come once one is ready. Oneness of humanity has to be ready to heal the part of the world they live. Animal and plant kingdom, Mother Earth is ready. Mankind it is time to ready yourselves and heal with Mother Earth and her vibrations or go into the oneness consciousness stream to be, for lack of better words, recycled. Those of you who choose will be ready and are ready now as she makes her final approaches into light and higher frequency of living. This is what you are preparing yourself for.

This has been the Galactic Federation speaking through use of Lia transmission.

In light and love,

Light Beings, Bringer of Light, ready yourself, as we love you

Why now? Why is love important in this day and age now?

Dear loved ones, you are all children of God. You must not deny your love from another soul. The love you give impacts everyone who exists. By loving, you open a space to clean the disharmony going on in the world today, the destruction across the world, the effect of your own environment and of your family.

Why is love needed now? Because without it all that you see will cease to exist. You are the same as your neighbor and he the same as the neighbor across the globe. Judgments are passed and you get lost in these words. It is not in these words that you will find the message, but in your heart. You must let go of the hurts and superiority roles. We are all one in the same. Forgive those who have wronged you and love them as a part of yourself. You hold on to this within your body and you will create more.

We have all wronged someone and hurt someone's feelings whether or not on purpose, child. This does not matter. The intent that this world needs now is love and forgiveness. Love like you have not ever loved and forgive as you never forgiven. You have the ability, the capability, to do all that I have done through a mindset of love. This world is changing by your actions and the Earth will continue to show her reaction.

Save the world you live on as it is your only home. Love yourself, your neighbor, the plants, and the animals, as you all coexist together and can help one another. Your love for you brother can heal your brother in need. The animals' love for humans can heal one by one. Through the power of divine love all that is not that in its presence must end or conform to love. You are this love.

With love,

Yod heh shin vav heh/Jesus

Compassion

Compassion for one another even if you do not understand will help you better relate to your peers. In life a compassionate heart is golden. Your views on each other are not. Have the willingness to accept that another is as they are. Without compassion you cannot know or understand love. Your heart must be willing to set the mind aside and just be. Take a moment to just feel with your heart a situation or interaction.

Love is all around you in all times but are you aware, loved ones? Do you have the compassion to understand that your peers journey is not yours but nor does it need your approval or judgment? Others who are suffering within themselves from their own battle of self love and compassion may say and do harsh things. But fear not. It is not your battle and no action is needed other than your unconditional love for one another and acceptance that the person needs not your retaliation, but love.

You need this same love. Give from a generous heart. Think with a clear mind and harmony will be a reality in this world. You cannot successfully coexist if you cease to accept your own existence in totality. Have compassion for yourself as you came here and this world is hard work. It is a school of higher education. It is the soul that will gain the riches of your deeds here so attach to this knowledge and not of the attachments of material. You are loved more than you know by a world both inside and outside of your own world. And this is our wish for you that you learn to love with a love divine and a compassion to understand you are all here working through this life together, one step at a time with many different journeys all at once.

It is with great love and compassion that I bid you love,

Quan Yin

The Archangels

Hello our fellow Earth angels. Our message to you is that you are never alone. We are always by your side, guiding you, loving you, and speaking to you by messages in everyday life. When you pray we hear you, when you speak and invoke us we are there. In tough transitions, with those of you in need, we strengthen our connection to those who interact. We love you dearly and are always at you side. There are many of us here. Some of which you learned about through schooling and other outlets given. There are more of us then you know and we are always assisting you.

Speak from your hearts, give from your hearts, and love from your hearts. Anything that is done with the heart as its foundation will succeed, will heal, and will make miracles happen and more so will bring together an entire world of people and species. Humanity had separated itself for many, many eons from others within their own population, and from other life forms. You are all connected and affected by one another. Love human angels beget love. The whole mission here is love—finding it, reconnecting to it, and experiencing it.

It will be your will and experiences that will bring you back to love divine. True love and light empowers and brings with it compassion and forgiveness. The largest test you will have this life is mastering your own being completely. Having control of your own mind, not another's. Loving yourself from within as it is not to be found outside of you. The people and situations around you mirror where you are with yourself and with one another. Uses this as a tool to aid you in this life. If there is something you see and it does not resonate with you, change this by going inside, accepting, acknowledging, and changing you.

This is a beautiful world you live in, with many freedoms only found here. You have the freedom to choose and create moment by moment. Choose love, Earth angels. At your center all of who you are is love. You are the highest love available. Your soul is ready to share this love with you and the world.

Quiet the mind and just be love. If only for a moment, sit in your heart center. That is where you will come to know all that ever was and will be. From the heart miracles will not be miracles but instead everyday happenings.

With deepest love and admiration,

We are the archangels

A Message from Gaia

Let me feed you with the life force you need. Let me revive you from the daily stresses you endure. Spend time in my majestic wonderland and be healed by its vibration. All that exist need me, and I am willing to share my existence with you. Are you willing to share what you take from me? Are you willing to love the land that you live on as though your life depended on it? Because it does. I have been in existence with you reincarnating and living here as I open my arms to you, precious ones.

I need from you as you need from me. I am not in a place of balance as a result of the lack of balance among you. This, precious one, boils down to an issue of self-love. Will you learn to love yourself, to maintain the existence of the planet you live? Just as you do, I, too, feel. I, too, need to maintain my own balance to aid each and every one of you. I am well aware and capable of how to realign and balance myself and you in your daily lives. Open to the frequency of love and healing of nature and my gifts and tools derived for your use.

Everything you need is already in place for you, waiting to be utilized by you, waiting for you to open your hearts and eyes a little wider. There are currently many of you trying to aid and better your existence and me through a greener route. I have taken notice and thank you kindly. It is an honor to be filled with such beautiful beings of light eager to make this place, to make this world better for you all that exist here.

But there are those who are not awake to the truths of what is going on in this planet. Right here in the very place you live. Out of sight out of mind? This is not true! You will still feel the repercussion of any harm done on any of this planet as you are all tied into one another including plants and animals. What you see here as natural disasters have been a result of shut eyes and closed minds. I have the strength, power, and the self-love necessary to heal myself and detoxify myself, and will do so.

As I speak, will you listen, precious ones? Will you awaken to the truth of what you turn your head to and allow in this existence and its harm that it causes all? Will you love yourself enough to treat yourselves and your world better? I am here. And we are one. Balance yourselves and you balance the world. It has been an honor sharing this transmission with you through another vessel of light. Lead proudly and confidently as you are never alone and adored.

With love from your Mother Earth,

Gaia

PART THREE

QUOTES FOR DAILY REFLECTION AND MEDITATION

This part of the book is a compilation of the many quotes and writings I co-wrote with angels, ascended masters, and God/Source. They are channeled messages for us all to remember who we are and that we are never alone in our journeys.

There is no right or wrong way to use this section. You will be divinely guided to what you need to read in each moment. Randomly open to a page, let your eyes fall where they may on that page and read your guided message for the day. Or you can start from page one and continue to the next page the following day. Let your soul guide you. It knows what it's doing. All it needs is you to listen.

Light, love, oneness.

The greatest form of art will always come from the heart.

Your body is art, so sculpt your masterpiece.

With change comes growth.

With growth comes wisdom.

With wisdom comes responsibility.

With responsibility comes love.

—God/Source

The eyes cannot hide the truth of the soul.

—Soul

How do you expect the flower to flourish to its best
capability if you don't take the time to nurture it,
to nourish it?

How is its blossom to be the healthiest it can be if there
is no time or effort taken to set it in the sun or give it the
water it needs?

How do you expect this flower to shine as your number
one if it always comes secondary in your life?

Flowers grow best in their proper environment.
Take the time to learn about the beauty, delicacy,
and nature of the flowers you choose and handle them
with care.

—Archangel Chamuel

Teach me, please don't lead me.

Break me, please don't lift me.

Love me, please don't idolize me.

I am here to experience who I am through the route
of compassion, love, understanding, and finally,
self-realization.

Honor the path of my light as I have honored the path
of yours.

—Leigh

The battle of what's right and what's wrong does not to be
justified by another.

Validation of your life's existence will not come
from another.

Your hurts, pains, and sorrows do not need permission
of another.

The circle of life does not require your belief in the process.

And Love, oh Love needs only the space.

—Archangel Chamuel

Trust that in each moment you are not alone and fully loved for the being that you are, totally and utterly.

—Soul

I am strong enough to cry when my heart aches from
the depths of my soul.

I am strong enough to apologize when I have faulted
and wronged another.

I am strong enough to take the fall because I know in falling
I rise.

I am strong enough to speak my truth though some may
not be able to handle it in its entirety.

I am strong enough to love with my heart wide open,
not putting regret, conditions, or strings on it,
so that you and I can both be free.

—Soul

Your destiny calls your heart.

Your fear calls your mind.

Which call will you answer?

—Pleiadians

How are you to let something wonderful in if you are holding onto the old that occupies your space?

In times that are not so wonderful, how are you to let something go if you will not let go of the clutter from the past?

In the stagnation of your current life, you say you want to change. But are you actively making changes and making room for change?

Or is it just quoted with junk in baggage that you don't use that you don't need and you don't even pay attention to you?

You cannot let in that love and happiness that you seek if you cannot let go of the pain, the baggage.

Make room for the new energy to flow that you ask for.

— Soul

Let go of the fears, worries, doubt, and seeking control of
that which is outside of yourself.

Forgive yourself and others who have wronged and hurt
you. Without forgiveness you can't fully let go,
fully experience the power that having trust in each
moment brings.

Love without attachments, dependencies, expectations,
and motives and experience a true love that is pure . . . not
of the head, but of the heart, from the soul.

This state of love will leave you full on all levels of
your being.

—God/Source

If the *eye* says a thousand words, then the tears tell its story: of what it has seen, what it has *endured,* and what the soul has become as a result.

The *tears* tell the journey of love *remembered* . . . love whole . . . love complete, love as *oneness.*

—Soul

You win when you realize the real fight is within not outside.

You win when you get past judging others and accepting that their truth may not be that of your truth and that this truth is acceptable for their journey.

You win when controlling another or a situation is not your goal or motive.

You win when you surrender to the healing, all-encompassing power of *love* . . . love in its true form of divinity and light . . . one love.

—God/Source

Flaws I've perfected my acceptance of them within myself.

Evolve.

Materialism, there is a fine balance of enjoyment we all deserve unless one feels they do not.

Spiritualism, I say the best spiritualists master themselves without forcing their views on another or feeling a being should be extreme one way or the other.

They look towards a greater Love Understanding and see the view from a higher place enabling the bigger picture.

Love is the beginning and the end and the glue that keeps us here as one.

—Leigh

If you played the game and knew beforehand that you would *win,* wouldn't that take the beauty, magic, raw growth, and fun out of the process of that *journey?*

Hmmmm. I think so.

Because there are so many different paths and choices, sometimes life is confusing.

But the choices are for each individual to choose.

Life is not right or left, black or white, unless you so choose.

And while we spend time judging what is right or wrong for another being we lose precious time in our own lives and waver off of our own paths.

If we each focus on love, being a better being, and not judging, but loving in acceptance of that which appears different, we are able to take the lead in our own lives.

This will affect the world as a whole by simply being present in our beautiful journeys in awareness.

—Soul

There is a difference between being lost in the confusion
of a moment and fully *living,* embracing, and *cherishing*
each *moment.*

There is an everlasting love that cannot be found in any
other moment but the here and now,
fully open and awake.

—Soul

Your happiness is dependent on *you.*
When the dependency of another to fulfill your state of
happiness subsides, you will achieve a happiness like no
other. You will find the frequency of you.

—Pleiadians

If you can't forgive and let go, how can you experience
love fully?

If you can't take the time to step out of your shoes into
another's, how are you to fully understand that your
perspective is not always the best for each individual?

If you can't use your words or actions to uplift,
then how are you to lead?

If you can't, how can you?

—Pleiadians

The importance of compassion is that it entails forgiveness,
understanding, and non-judgment while allowing your heart
to fully open, to give and receive love as not only you know
it to be, but as another has learned to give.

—Moses

Obstacles to succumb in your *life*, destinations award
you the chance to see how beautiful a soul and *resilient*
you truly are.

With these hurdles you are taught strength believe in you.

—Archangels

Filtering the mind and one's words will not better
them or you.

The lesson is in learning to allow them to be unfiltered as
the truth will be shown to them of where their awareness is
and needs to be.

And the lesson for you is to relinquish control, because this
will set your mind free and allow your heart to take over.

This is your center, so allow yourself to open up to the
vulnerability of heart. It needs no protection,
but expression.

It needs no protection, but free expression,
allowing your soul to feel, to live, and to be vulnerable even
if it's uncomfortable, brings you to know true,
all-encompassing love.

Let go of the stigma and let love, let the heart just *breathe.*

—Moses

If you never tried how would you know you had the ability?

If you never took risks how would you have known the impossible was *possible?*

If you would not have given selflessly how would you have known the impact this *selflessness* had on others?

And if you did not *encounter* people and situations in life which required you to *love* yourself and others *unconditionally,* how would you have known that love, yes *love,* is the greatest gift you can give to yourself and others?

How would you have known this and *more* if you did not?

—Archangels

Have you ever noticed the petals of a flower as
they blossom?

They start off closed and sheltered as a bud, then one by
one they open with excitement of *growth* in awe of their
new form once they have reached full *attainment*.

Though the petals, each one with its unique character,
as shown by shades, curls, and markings not found on the
others, one thing remains the same.

They are connected at the base, where they
originally started.

They are still one.

They are still love.

—Moses

Remember *yesterday,* for it holds lessons learned
in the past.

Relish today for in these moments you define your
character and *create* your future.

When given the chance to *love,* love without conditions.
It is the *purest* form of love.

When your *belief* is tested by the world, *believe* even more.

There will be tests to see if you can *withstand* the odds.

When given the choice of being your *authentic self* or
the self pretended to be, honor the real you knowing that
authentic cannot be duplicated and therefore is *invaluable.*

Choose to see life's truths and *truth* will be shown.

—Archangels

Life is not race to see who can get there first.

Life is a *journey* filled with a path of roses and mountains to bring you back to the essence of the *divine.*

Taking *complete* responsibility of lessons in your life drawn toward you for your journey *empowers.*

Harness this power by experiencing each moment to its fullest, knowing it brings you back to love on *all* levels.

—Soul

Speak from the heart; your words are *golden,*

Give from the heart; your touch is *Midas.*

Love from the heart; love's vibration will be felt through the diamond web of life for *eternity.*

—Soul

Your path will be lit with the *illumination* of a higher love and truth.

When the feeling of joy, love, and light are felt in your heart by actions chosen by you, you will know without doubt that this path is for you.

Everyone has a path unique to growth needed for each to bring one back to the original state of love and full acceptance of who you are as well as acceptance of others as they are.

—Soul

One of life's many gifts to you is *joy.*

More than a feeling it is an *experience* awaiting you.

How to receive this gift is with arms wide open fully embracing life and all that life entails while being centered in the *heart.*

—Archangels

There is a kindness, gentleness, and innocence in all that
can only be seen by those with *childlike eyes.*

Wash clean, free from judgment, to see the rainbow of love
that exists in all.

—Jesus

Self-belief is crucial to reaching small and large successes
in life. Your *belief* in you empowers.

This belief is more powerful than the words of those who
do not believe.

Move *forward,* trusting that there is a bigger plan.

Even if at that *moment* it is not foreseen and actions
of others not fully understood.

—God/Source

The best way to soar is to jump in *freely,* filled with belief, hope, and knowing you can do what others said was impossible.

—Soul

If you turn away from that which you fear, your lesson has not been learned.

Thus repetition until the *self*-realization and knowledge that you are strong, you are courageous, and you are love is fully *recognized and actualized.*

Compassion and sincerity are not characteristics that can be mimicked.

They are rooted in the soul and radiate through the heart and eyes.

—Soul

Hold steadfast to the belief, feeling, and knowing that your
needs and desires in life are met.

Then follow as your heart leads.

The art of *manifestation.*

Triumph comes when you look obstacles in the in the eyes
and *graciously* move through them.

—Soul

Take flight in life by allowing yourself to be who you
already are.

You are success.

You are love.

—Soul

Everything happens in *divine* time and as it should for that moment.

When you continue on your path of growth doors must close to reveal the *gifts* reaped from that growth.

—Soul

Love *all* of yourself totally and utterly.

Denying any part of you leaves a feeling of being unbalanced.

There is beauty and love in the perfect creation of who you are.

—Archangels

Laughter, it *heals,* releases, and keeps you in the
moment—exactly where you need to be to enjoy
life to the fullest.

—Archangel Uriel

Open your heart to giving and receiving *love.*

Pay attention to what ways love has entered into your day,
be that big or small.

Then show *gratitude* for the gift that comes freely from one
soul to another.

—Archangels

Love's light cannot be over shadowed even in darkness.

Its power is *infinite*.

Its flame is *eternal*.

Even when there is trickery, love's light and love's truth cannot be hidden.

—Soul

It is when we break the mold of what we have been taught by society and we relearn from within that we reach new *heights* in ourselves and in life.

—Soul

Allowing yourself to show vulnerability is a sign of strength.

Only the strong can share their sadness, heartaches, and, yes, tears with the world.

For they know that this is not a sign of weakness, but the movement of love, compassion, and humility in a being of greatness.

—Soul

Through the self we learn to *breathe* deep again.

Through the self we learn to *give* again.

Through the self we learn *trust* again.

Through the self we learn to be *selfless* again.

Through the self we learn to be what we already are again.

Love love love.

—Archangel Jophiel

In random acts of kindness, unspoken *respect* for mankind is shown, thus unveiling the domino effect of love and remembrance of our inner connection, *our oneness.*

—Jesus

The epitomes of peace, love, joy, beauty, and all those things you search for in life are *within you.*

Searching outside of yourself will leave you with a feeling of emptiness.

You are whole.

—Oneness Consciousness

May you be free from the limitations of the mind into the
vastness of the oneness you are.

—Archangels

Liberate yourself from boundaries set forth by others
by being, by allowing yourself just to be in your own
awareness of who you are in your entirety along with
your *divine* capabilities.

—Archangels

Each key emits a note that is in harmony with the key next to it, be that up or down.

This is much like the steps we take in life to achieve our goals.

Each step is in *harmony* with the next, be that a step forward or backward, to bring the growth needed for each individual.

—Archangel Gabriel

Today is a new day filled with new adventures, new opportunities, and new experiences defining who you are: courageous, beautiful, strong, true, love, and whole.

—Archangels

Life is not black and white.

Step out of your box, out of your comfort zone.

You will see yourself, others, and the vivid rainbow of
beauty and opulence of the world we live in.

—Soul

Loving without strings attached and without expectations
brings the soul its true rewards.

The core of who you are and who you have always been
is *love*.

Love is free.

—Archangel Chamuel

Art done in great love and *passion* leaves the most memorable impact in our mind and on our hearts.

Life is living *art*.

—Archangel Uriel

Love love love is truly what makes the world go round.

It is the *connection* that keeps us linked at our deepest level, the *soul*.

—Oneness consciousness

Every battle is not yours to fight.

Know when to stand *strong* in the current position you are
in and know when to move *boldly* forward in love.

—Soul

Cherish the journey of life and all it has to offer.

Those moments are *memories* that cannot be replaced
or duplicated in its entirety.

—Soul

Attempting to hold another person back when you have
the ability to help holds you back.

What you do in life comes back *full circle.*

Take steps actions that lead to the betterment of others
which leads to the betterment of you.

—Soul

Stand on the other side of the window and take the view
from the outside in.

If you are looking to make a *positive* change you need a
clear understanding and more than one angle.

—Soul

Life passes you by when you assume it's just a game.

Life is *fulfilling* once you realize that each moment you are given the chance to love, learn, trust, give, forgive and believe.

Walk in truth and just *be*.

—Archangel Uriel

Acceptance and honoring differences in one another makes *coexisting* in peace and harmony possible.

—Archangels

You were meant to have a life of happiness defined by you.

If that means treasures in the form of material goods that add to your happiness, it is okay.

Just do not allow your goods to define who you are.

Balance in both spiritual and material is possible so long as your *foundation* is built and backed by love.

—Soul

Blessings surround every situation in life.

It's up to you to notice and *appreciate* those daily blessings.

By taking notice and being grateful, you *allow* more to flow to you.

—Soul

Learn to control your tongue and actions and know when
the time is right to be golden with *silence* or golden in
speaking your truth.

The people you consider your foes are teachers here
to help you learn *self-mastery* and unconditional love for
one another.

—Soul

The road toward reaching your *life goals* is worth
the journey.

The view you get from actualizing that accomplishment
is *breathtaking.* Bringing in a sense of gratification,
accomplishment, and joy achieved by you.

You are what *dreams* are made of.

Fulfill your dreams.

—Soul

Lead the way and be the candle that *illuminates* the path
in darkness.
Do not sabotage another.
Uplift them in love and know you cannot stop light that is
meant to shine from illuminating.

—Archangels

Love . . . it is our *life force.*
It starts with you, with self-love.
For some, it's the missing piece of the puzzle.
For others, it is the glue that keeps life filled with *beauty,*
peace, and *wonder.*

—Archangel Uriel

Reaching the top of any mountain takes your hard work,
your dedication, and your belief in you and your
unlimited *capabilities*.

Do not limit yourself with other people's boundaries and
disbelief of their own *magnificence*.

—Soul

Being jealous of others shows an inadequacy within you
that needs to be *healed*.

Wish others love, success, and good will.

By doing so, you attract these into your own life.

—Soul

The funny thing about growing up from childhood
to adulthood is that you sometimes forget you still have
a lot to *learn.*

You never stop learning or reach an age where you know
everything there is to know, love, and appreciate in life.

Don't close yourself off to the knowledge and the wonders
in life because you think you know all there is to know.

Even from the little ones in your life wisdom can be gained,
lessons can be learned.

—Archangels

Look in the *eyes* if you want to see the truth.

Listen with your inner *ears* if you want to hear the truth.

Feel the words in your *heart* if you want to know the truth.

—Archangel Gabriel

May you light up the world with the *love, beauty,*
and *knowledge* that you share with me every day.

You are beautiful, you are grand, and you are love
in action.

—Soul

A laugh can create *joy* in someone's heart,

Bring a *sparkle* to someone's eyes,

And prompt a *smile* from the deepest part of us all . . .

The soul.

—Archangel Uriel

Life may be *humbling,* yet it is also *rewarding.*

Life lifts you up when the time is needed and blesses you with lessons to remind you of who you are.

You are greatness, you are love, and it is your divine right to succeed in life.

—Archangels

The choice to be who you are in every *moment* is entirely up to you and the actions you choose to take.

—Soul

Ride the waves of gratitude.

Having sincere *gratitude* for who you are and the blessings in your life ushers in more *abundance*.

—Archangels

Trust, your destiny awaits you.

The *journey* to become who you are meant to be in this life begins with you taking the first leap of faith in you.

—Soul

Life is now.

Now provides us with *moments.*

Each new moment provides us with a chance to live
and love fully, positively impacting ourselves and those
around us.

The moment is yours.

How will you spend it?

—Soul

Walking in *light* does not mean that you will not walk
through the darkness.

What it means is that you will be able to walk within *your*
light unfalteringly.

—Archangels

Compromising allows you to be true to yourself while honoring the *truth* of another.

Loving compromises are the key to producing *harmonious* relations.

—Soul

Compassion makes *coexistence* possible.

Though we have differences, one love keeps us connected in pure, divine, and *unconditional love.*

—Oneness consciousness

Dance to the rhythm of life and be free.

Allow your soul to conduct the music of your heart as it can only come from *within*.

—Archangel Haniel

True smiles come from *soul* and are felt through the *heart*.

False smiles are *transparent*.

Which smile do you choose to share with the world today?

—Soul

By letting you go, it shows that I love you,
I accept you as you are, and I respect the light in *you*
which connects with the light in *me* that has given me
so much growth and wisdom.

—Soul

How is one to know what is in your heart if you keep it
locked inside?

Speak that which is in your heart so your message can be
heard and your words can be *felt*.

—Archangels

There is something *special* inside of each and every individual that must be unlocked in order to pursue and define their *happiness*.

—God/Source

By loving and accepting the parts of ourselves we consider imperfections we are able to *truly* love and accept those imperfections in others—and to recognize those parts make us *whole*.

—Archangels

Don't always hide underneath the umbrella when it rains.

You do not have to fear the thunderstorms in your life.

It is during these times when you are able to see the
strength and beauty of the spirit that you are.

Embrace the rain, as with it comes growth.

—Archangels

Your world is created by where you hold your *thoughts*.

What you focus on.

Take the focus off of being negative and critical and focus
more on *love, acceptance, kindness* and being whole.

—Soul

Words are like a rainbow that can fill someone's day with happiness, joy, and heal the soul with *light and love.*

Be the best authentic and original you in this world.

Not a copy of someone you wish to be.

But the *masterpiece* of who you are.

—Soul

If you think the grass appears greener on the other side, it is because the gardener of that grass is tending to it.

Tend to your garden with *love* and it will be just is green.

—Soul

You will not agree 100 percent of the time with everything you see or hear.

Nor are you supposed to.

The difference in thought of one another is there to strike a fire in you to go *inward* and trust.

Your way is not better than another's.

All paths lead to the same destination in the end.

Step back without judgment and see the *bigger picture*.

—Soul

The *cycles* in your life that you complain about will continue until you realize you have the power to *choose* differently.

Align the mind, body, and soul with love and watch your world *transform*.

—Oneness consciousness

Forgiveness is needed to *let go*.

Letting go is needed to bring *resolve*.

Resolve is one of the many ingredients that is needed to bring *inner peace* and *self-love*.

—Jesus

Let your inner child out today.

Remember what it feels like to be fearless and carefree.

—Soul

Through the eyes of love, you see the clearer picture.

Choose the *light*.

—Soul

There is *beauty* in all.

Once you choose to focus on this truth the ego's judgment
will fall obsolete.

—Archangels

Inward in silence is reflected your true nature,
your true beauty.

You are *love*.

—God/Source

Love takes us to new heights and unlocks doors we never imagined . . . *believe.*

—Soul

Fire can ignite a *flame* in the heart to *heal* or an explosion in the *mind* to *corrupt.*

Choose wisely.

—Buddha

At times, love speaks softly only to be *felt* by the heart and *remembered* by the soul.

—Archangel Chamuel

Let love be the force that moves you,

Wisdom be the knowledge that guides you,

Light and conviction be what keep you not unbendable,

But *unbreakable* on your path.

—Archangel Gabriel

The petals of flowers are individually beautiful and *unique*.

Each petal is needed to make the flower whole.

Just as each person, animal, and plant, with its differences make this world we live in *whole*.

It is *oneness*.

—Oneness consciousness

With truth comes *freedom*.

Sometimes hearing the truth alone is enough.

Other times truth must be looked straight in the eyes for its *power* to be felt.

—Soul

You are more than your physical body.

Explore and reconnect with your inner self and experience love again.

—Soul

Self-mastery is achieved by taking a higher point of view and seeing through the *inner* eyes with love.

—Archangels

You are *perfect* in this moment.

Accept and love all of yourself.

Without the *yin* and *yang* dualities of your being,
you would not exist.

—Soul

The path is yours to walk.

Choose that which resonates with your inner being and not
that which is chosen for you by another.

—Archangels

The gift of *free will* is in each moment.

We are free to choose one action over another, one path over another.

Guidance will always be there awaiting you without pressure to help you walk in your light.

—Archangels

Life is like a well-tuned piano.

Every step you take is a musical composition beautifully played and orchestrated by your choices and actions to bring you back to your original state of *love*.

—Archangel Jophiel

The only medicine you need to fill the feeling of void is *love.*

—Archangels

There is a *light* within every heart waiting to be
rediscovered, *remembered,* revealed.

—Archangels

Love is the beginning and the end.

The experiences in between is the *journey* that brings you to and from this original state.

—God/Source

Love requires you being receptive to the *truth*,
letting go even if it hurts and *understanding* that everything happens for a divine reason as it is intended to happen.

There is a bigger picture.

Trust.

—Soul

You are given a choice in every moment to walk your path of light.

Life gives you many opportunities to break free from fear-based actions and claim your full power.

The choice is always yours.

Choose love.

—Soul

Love is a colorful *gift*.

Free someone today by showing them the beauty of a *pure love* that's unconditional and divine.

—Soul

You are never alone.

Even in darkness your shadow still remains, you just need the light's illumination.

It's there.

Because you do not see does not mean it does not *exist*.

—Archangels

Compassion brings you to a place of love through understanding and empathy.

When people have reached this place in their being the words "we are *one*" are much more than words with a meaning not fully understood.

There now exist the *conscious connection* of the body, mind, and soul in motion.

—Oneness consciousness

Believe in yourself and what you are *capable* of.

Surround yourself with those who wish you *happiness and success.*

Show those who think the impossible is impossible, what the *power of belief* can do.

—Soul

When we live aligned with our highest purpose, success is inevitable.

—Soul

Extraordinary are those who choose to give their best performances in life and experiences with the expectation none other than to be a light of luminance in the darkness of illusion and hatred.

—Jesus

Free yourself from the thoughts of others.

What you *create* needs only your belief to be stronger than their fear of your success.

—Soul

Flower petals, when falling from the flower, are still as miraculously beautiful as they were when they were in a flower ensemble.

There comes a time when to be the greatest and most individual petal, the petal must fall away from the group and lead from the *light within.*

—Archangel Chamuel

The best path is the authentic one, the one that is true to who you are without compromise and full acceptance of the greatness inside of you.

When you stop searching for answers, acceptance, and love outside of yourself and focus, clearly see your final destination, the path will fully open up to you as it awaits your footsteps, your mark to leave on this world.

—WWTA

Be true to yourself on your journey this life.

Honor, love, and accept all life throws at you.

For without the tests and belief in yourself how were you to know how great you are?

Do not run; just walk in awe of the beautiful moments that allow you to see your true self in life's experiences.

—Soul

Being physically strong does not make you a champion.

It is heart that makes a champion.

Through all the trials, letdowns, and what seemed to be losses, when your inner strength or your belief was questioned, you still stood like a light.

You knew that in that moment you were a champion because you never gave up, never stayed down, and stayed true to the vision inside of your heart without compromising for those who did not believe.

Only a champion can stand in the midst of the highest odds.

—Archangels

If you knew you held the key to happiness,
would you unlock the door?

If you knew you had the tools for success,
would utilize those tools?

If you knew that love was waiting for your acknowledgment
and staring right back at you would you acknowledge it?

It's all found there in each moment and not found in others,
but inside of you reflected in others.

This is your journey.

Make it a symphony of beautiful, miraculous moments.

—WWTH

The destination is *love.*

The journey is *growth.*

The consciousness is *oneness.*

—Soul

Playfully jump into the garden of life.

Bask in the different colors, scents, and experiences
it brings.

With each new endeavor you try, remember who you are
as this will lead you to who you were meant to *be.*

—Soul

To make yourself empty is to make yourself *full*.

Let go of the emptiness of attachments and control and let the *lightness of love* instead leave your soul full.

—Soul

When your internal fight ends, your external flight begins.

—Soul

When we take challenges head on we reap the rewards of being so bold.

Like when you climb to the top of the mountain and submerge yourself in the challenges of climbing upward.

The journey might get you a little bit dirty, a little bit tired, but once you reach that top you see beauty that could not have been seen until you arrived at that spot.

This is where all the little steps taken brought you to a wonderful sight in picture-perfect view.

Live your life not in agony of the climb, but in wonder and awe of how each of your steps led to the biggest step . . . seeing the grand view from the point of attainment.

—Soul

When I close my eyes, through my eye, I see the color of
the rainbow emanating from every part of creation.

I see the energy of love as light and feel it as a musical
note with a range of frequency higher than what the human
mind alone is able to fathom.

Its sound of love is sung by a choir of angels and its scent
is like the smell of a saltwater ocean breeze as it kisses a
soft and delicate rose. If I had to name its resonance,
it would be om.

—Soul

The heartfelt intent, or emotion, that went into choosing a
gift just for you is the real *treasure*.

—God/Source

It is not the material you truly seek, it is the feeling you get once that material object is in your hand that you are looking for.

Know that this feeling, this emotion can be accessed by *feeling gratitude* in each moment for all that you have and *all* that you do not have.

—God/Source

It is not the treasures you acquire that define you.

It is in knowing who you are *authentically* and *accepting* this *truth* about who you really are in *unconditional love* that makes and defines you.

—God/Source

When we realize it is not about the win, who is better, or who has more, we reach a space within ourselves that makes room for the divine *unification* and *realization* that life is more than . . . relationships are more than . . . and our status in the eyes of ourselves are more than superficial.

We are *love,* we are *greatness,* we are *one.*

—God/Source

Teach or show others who need your guidance the way, but let them choose and live their lives without the pressure of yours.

That responsibility is not yours.

Their lessons are their own for fulfilling and accepting.

—Archangels

Beauty surrounds you at all time.

Let your senses envelop you in these wonderful
experiences without hesitation about what is next.

Beauty is found being present.

—Archangel Jophiel

You are the water . . . flow.

You are the leaves in the wind . . . dance.

You are the sun and the moon . . . balance.

You are all in oneness . . . love.

—God/Source

An open mind makes for the perfect vessel of light.

—God/Source

When we trust we allow the natural flow.

When we give without expectation we allow the freedom that comes from true gifts.

When we forgive and let go we allow the presence of a *love unconditional.*

—God/Source

Why blame when you choose experiences?

Why blame when what you see is a reflection of you that
seeks your acceptance and healing *love?*

Why blame when you have the power to change
everything by changing one: *you.*

—God/Source

Hurt and pain do not lessen, nor do they disappear,
by running away.

Your pains and hurts of the past held onto can be the
vessel that pushes the joy and love away in your
present moments.

You cannot live in the now, in this moment, if you are stuck
in the scenes from yesterday.

Your mind will not allow.

But if you go within your heart, yesterday is a memory of
experiences you've lived, loved, forgiven, yet not forgotten.

Your *heart* grounds you in the moment with all its
wonderful possibilities of surrendering to the movement
of *love* in the *present.*

—God/Source

The act of *divine* service from one being to another is a gift from the highest part of you.

It is the souls honor and true nature to give freely and love unconditionally for the highest good of all.

—Archangel Ariel

But the most *precious* part of self-discovery is remembering and deciphering the illusion from *truth,* going from uncertainty to *certainty,* lack thereof to more than enough, being incomplete to *knowing* you have always been *complete* and from moving from a state of self-hate, which is reflected in the world you see before you, back to the *authentic* state of love reflected in the *heart of the soul.*

—Archangel Ariel

Freeing yourself from the rapture of another's thoughts into the thoughts of the inner being of yourself brings you to victory on the road to the truth of you, authentically.

—Archangel Ariel

Love's truth, though it is reflected in your outer world, is found in the chambers of your heart.

The search ends and the answers begin within.

—Archangel Chamuel

Though you seek for attention from those around you,
it is your heart that seeks the attention from you.

The void you are seeking to fill will not be filled with those
around you lest temporary.

The void is self-love and until you know how radiantly
beautiful you are and accept all that you are from the inside
there will always be a void.

It is your inner self that seeks your love and acceptance,
and until you go in you will feel without.

—Archangel Chamuel

It has *always* been you.

You are *love.*

Don't you see it when you look into to the eyes of another?

Don't you *feel* it in the loving embrace of a friend or family?

Don't you *taste* it in the meals of your favorite entrees?

Don't you *smell* it in in the perfume of nature's air when
you breathe?

Don't you *hear* it in the rhythmic melodies of the music?

Dear ones, *love is all* around you, inside of you.

It is what you are made of.

You are the beauty of love's might.

It is reflected everywhere around you.

It's reflected everywhere *inside of you.*

—Galactic Federation

The greatest parts of who I am are my infinite connections
to more than me, all of me, and my heart connection to all
that I have ever been and will become in the memories of
one heart one mind, one consciousness.

—Leigh

Where do you put your focus when before you lays a beautiful, fully blossomed bundle of flowers encircled with what appears as nonliving evergreens?

Is your attention held on the beautiful flowers or is it on the plant that appears to be nonliving?

If your gaze is left on the plants that appear to be an inclusion in your view of the beautiful flowers,
you are mistaken, for they are not an inclusion and are alive and well.

Their season (time of blossom) is not here yet.

But when this season comes, the blossom is just as beautiful as the flowers you so adore.

It's kind of like a Phoenix rising in rebirth.

There is a blissful *balance* that is captivated in the entire scene as a *whole.*

—Archangel Uriel

Life isn't translucent, your *emotions* are.

It is here you will find access to what stuck inside of you
and it is here where you can face and heal your *heart,*
your *body,* and your *mind.*

—Archangel Uriel

Your *inner* wisdom holds your *truth.*

Sitting still, being inside of you, you come to know you
from the perspective of your soul and this is the key to
victory of the *self.*

—Archangel Uriel

You have the power to break free,
to *change* and choose differently.

You have the power to *forgive* and *love* fully.

You have the power walk, eyes wide *open,*
and to have *heart* without fear.

You have the power to be *you.*

You have the power to be *you.*

—Archangel Uriel

I read a story once and grasped the beauty of the journey.

I read a story twice and grasped the wisdom of its words.

I read that same story a third time and fell in love with the
silent chorus that sung to my *heart.*

—God/Source

I saw the leaves' radiance from the beauty of the sun's golden light shining down on them.

I saw diamond light dance upon the water as the suns golden light shone down to kiss the ocean.

I saw the light of all existence fill the spaces of doubt within your heart so that your being could fill the space of doubt in many others.

—God/Source

Performing daily tasks does not compare to performing tasks of the *inner self*.

To love yourself is to know yourself. To know yourself is to love yourself in *totality*.

—Archangel Jophiel

When you are able to find the beauty of the soul within yourself, you are able to notice the beauty of the souls that come across your path every day.

If you seek a true connection from your heart to another's heart you will see that the physical and mental differences didn't make one better than another.

The differences were the balance you needed for your experience in the moment of nonjudgmental love . . . *unconditional love.*

—Archangel Jophiel

When you make it to that beautiful rainbow, will you have cherished the journey to the rainbow or just the rainbow?

Your experiences on the way gave the rainbow that shines that magnificent color.

Because with each step you took your light, grew bright, shone stronger, and move more fluid in connection to love's vibration.

You created the rainbow.

If it was not for your choice, your belief, and your actions, that rainbow would not be there.

—Archangel Jophiel

We are one in a symphony of all the majestic colors produced by the sound of music.

Your note completes the song; it is your note that harmonizes the melody and your note that brings us home, into the blissful sonata of oneness.

—Archangel Jophiel

All that is exists in the present moment.

Placing your thoughts and focusing your energy be that stuck in the past or projecting what you wish for the future ceases the beautiful and miraculous experiences to be felt in the present.

It is here.

It is in the *now* that you create who you are and experience all that you are when fully enveloped in the moments.

It is here where you power to transform your world and the world you live to a higher state of being to its destination and unification of oneness where we are all self realized oneness, where we find the nature of who we are . . . love.

—Archangel Uriel

The best choice for those you care deeply about is that
you live according to your *truth*, your higher self.

By doing so you allow others to choose what is in
their highest good in any given moment just by your state
of being.

—Archangel Uriel

Follow the path of your heart and you will be all that you are
and all that you are destined to be.

Follow the path of another's heart you will live the
standards another's truth lost in an illusion.

—Archangel Uriel

The footsteps on the ground before you were left to remind you not to follow another's blueprint or map of life and its destinations.

They are there cemented to remind you to leave your own miraculous footprints for those who come behind you to see the *golden* journey of one soul's truth, one soul's light, one soul's mission, so they too can ignite the spark of life of love within themselves.

—Archangel Uriel

This morning as I drove, I looked out of my rearview mirror and saw a beautiful sight: the sun, in all its golden beauty, rising above the clouds.

This reminded me of a saying about leaving the past behind you to move forward.

After reflecting on this stunning image of the sun rising behind me, I thought I should add this message to the book.

While we move forward and let go of the past, if we take responsibility for the past and let go, not in anger, bitterness, or even resentment, we will see that the past is a gift of beautiful lessons not to hold onto, but to let go of, grow from, and to take notice of the better *you* the experience produced.

All experiences lead to you remembering you, with a choice of owning who you are, the power within you, and the gift of showing others who they are through your interactions amongst one another.

There is a *light* that yearns to grow brighter, to *illuminate* the truth of you if only you choose to experience the beauty and miracles that stem from situations and people instead of choosing blame or lack of owning your actions.

You are love and each action, whether or not you see it in the moment, leads to *love* at your completion.

—Leigh

The breath of life.

The golden key to life is in a breath of life.

In this breath you restore, make new, and recycle.

As you inhale you breathe in perfect harmony, love,
and *vitality*.

As you exhale, you recycle all that is no longer needed in
your life, your body, your energy.

The more you focus on the breath and the deeper the
breath is in that moment, the more you connect to the
wholeness and innate love of the inner being,
the *divine being* you are.

You were given the gifts to be all that you desire to be.

You are not powerless, but powerful.

This is realized by breathing, deepening the breath of life.

—God/Source

You play the part, but do you live the role?

Let go of the limitations of the mind, of others beliefs, of your own fear.

Awaken to the limitless opportunities, moments that allow you to be sa you desire to become.

It is inside of you.

Live you from the inside out instead of outside of yourself and attempting to force this within.

You can only be who you are.

You are love and greatness from the inside out.

The key is within, this is who you are.

Radiate it outward beautiful ones.

—God/Source

Have you ever noticed the winds as it blew through you,
past you, around you?

At times the force may be gentle and other times harsh,
but nonetheless it flows in a complete harmony within itself.

It knows its beauty and all its might.

It is unstoppable in forward motion until it has reached its
destination or chosen to surrender to the tides of a love
that brings them back into balance of a higher wholeness,
a unity of *oneness*.

—God/Source

In stillness, we see the movement of our words,
our thoughts, and our actions played out before us.

It is a choice to be free, a choice to be what you thought
you were unable of.

On the sideline of each story are those who wish to see
the book not completed.

This is not your worry, but theirs.

Yours is a masterpiece destined to be.

You mustn't worry about the insurmountable.

This is an illusion.

This is fear.

When you change lenses, change perspective, and gain
perfect clarity of your goal and your path to take the fear,
the illusion, and what you once considered insurmountable
is yours to conquer.

It is then surmountable.

—Ganesh

If you knew that the wall that stands before you made of
stone would crumble at the slightest touch of the force not
brought about through your hands but through the *will* of
your *heart,* would you believe in the magic, beauty,
and greatness of who you are no matter what appears in
front of your eyes?

You have the power, you have the strength,
and it rests *within* your heart.

The heart of a warrior.

—Ganesh

The challenge is not the obstacle you feel is before you.

It is but the one and only obstacle you have that blocks you, belief in who you are and what you are truly capable of.

If you think for a moment you are capable of what others say you or they are capable of, you shut yourself off to the *limitless* beauty, wisdom, knowledge, and strength you came into this world with.

Expand your knowledge of yourself by letting your soul guide direct and reteach you all that you are in *oneness*.

—Ganesh

The belief is that you need to protect your heart
and emotions.

To the contrary, what you call protecting brings resistance.

It is a wall or defense mechanism you have learned to
shield yourself from hurt.

Truth be told, this puts you in a constant place of fear and
being on the defensive.

This wall you put up does not allow you to let love in in all
its forms.

Sometimes love is found in a lesson that draws you
inward due to an experience, teaching you to value the
love that you are and to live from that fountain that streams
inside of you.

The pain that you feel is needed so that you know what
experiences resonate with you and what you wish to
create in the next moment that brings you closer to your
authentic self.

—Archangel Michael

Authentically you are vulnerable, how else would you empathize or have compassion?

Authentically you are fearless, how else would you be able to choose to experience and create that in your life which brings the feeling of pain?

Authentically you are the most magnificent love ever created by the highest purest orchestrator in existence, but how who you came to know and understand this in all the depths of your being if you never chose to open to the oneness, the connection you have to all things if you didn't journey inward?

—Archangel Michael

By choosing to be bold, by choosing to be you in each moment, you allow the internal light to shine out into the world.

This light of great illumination cannot be denied by those with eyes wide open and its radiance is one that even the greatest magicians cannot recreate to the exact blueprint.

What makes this world go round is *love,* and this is what unites you to all. This is where true illumination is born.

—Archangel Michael

Feel free from the chaos.

Feel free from worries and doubts.

Move into your center, into your being,
and pull from this place.

You create from within and cycles of perceived
disharmony in your life end and subside when you are
seated in your center.

Stand in your light.

You are ready now, dear child, and we all dearly love and
support you.

It has been such a wonderful honor to see you grow,
dear child. It is now time for you to stand tall in your power,
your god self.

It is who you are.

Releases the fear practice, as you are always divinely
guided and protected.

In love, dearest, from us all.

—Archangel Ariel

Freedom surrenders control, judgments, and separation.

You are only free when you *let go.*

Live fully and do without expectations.

You are your greatest manifestation this life and given the gift of creating and recreating in each moment *flow, be love.*

Who are you today?

What will you create as your experiences to define your being?

Will you recreate an existence you have outgrown or will you create experiences that are driven by the soul in alliance and *harmony* with all.

Let go and just be experience your true nature . . . *unconditional love* without boundaries, expectations, or judgments.

Now is the time.

This moment is yours.

—Archangel Ariel

If I smiled a thousand smiles,
at first sight you would *see* my joy.

If I smiled a thousand smiles,
at second sight you would *feel* my life's journey.

If I smiled a thousand smiles,
at third sight you would come to *know* my victory,
my story of self-love unified in *oneness.*

—Archangel Ariel

There is a path that calls your name.

This is the path where you will shine and excel.

It is in harmony with the pattern of your soul and the frequency of your *heart*.

You ask, but do not listen to the answers that are provided inside of you.

You instead choose to listen to answers of that outside of you.

Your path awaits you.

Listen to the melody as it calls to you from *within*.

—Archangel Ariel

Close your eyes, for what you need to see cannot be seen
with the physical eyes.

Close your ears for what you need to hear can only be
heard from your internal ears through silence.

Close your mouth for the words which need be spoken
speak from the heart and need no words to accompany
the depths of what spoken by means of feeling.

If what you have done is not working, stop and this time
just *be,* without force feel the *flow* of you in *stillness.*

It is here that you are whole and have
everything necessary.

—Archangel Ariel

Roads are built and some even crumble.

The shoe that fits (the *you* that fits) is the one created and remembered by you and not the one made by another and given to you.

The map to your true path has always been inside of you, but can only be shown to you when you are ready.

When you step back inside of yourself and realize the shoe given to you by another is built according to their map, their journey, you can see it is only an option for you to experience this if you choose.

—God/Source

When we deem a road foreseen only from our eyes the correct and true path for all, we lose sight of all the little pieces of creation and experiences that make us whole, *connected.*

—God/Source

The butterfly with a piece of its wing missing does not stop flying. The butterfly continues to flutter its wings gracefully.

It sees the missing piece not as a scar caused by life's conditions, but a visual gift to remind her where she's been and how much stronger and higher it forced her to learn how to fly on her own, conquering new heights.

—Archangels

Having the knowledge of wholeness without credit to all the aspects, all the tiny parts that makes this a whole, is futile if the time is not taken to open up to the reality that more exists outside the one you currently know.

There are more ways than the one way you see, and all are correct in every given moment for all.

You cannot come to know a whole without seeking to awaken your eyes to intricacy of the small pieces that currently complete this whole.

—Leigh

When we fight against who we are, instead of surrendering to the love that we are, we recreate chaos outside of ourselves and have no one to blame but ourselves if we don't like it.

—Leigh

Let the light of your heart, your soul, and your being shine bright in truth.

Not in truth of another's words or perceptions, but in the truth of who you know yourself to be.

People will see what they are capable of seeing and what is needed for them to see for their own inner growth.

—Archangels

If you cannot see love in the most simplistic forms and actions in life, in the fear, in the doubt, in all the little things, how are you to notice love in yourself?

How are you to notice when a small gesture of *love* is made, how are you to *feel* the love that comes after the pain, and in all change, if you cannot/will not see and are not *open*.

—Leigh

If silence spoke, it would sing a melody to your heart.

—Leigh

The peaceful journey is not one without noise or kept within a comfort zone.

The peaceful journey is in the stillness of your heart even when sailing on treacherous waters.

The soul follows its own rhythm, and the mind the rhythm of what it was taught.

Combine the two and you have harmony.

—Leigh

Let the *light* shine on the *shadow* of who you are so that you can come to a place to embrace and accept this part of yourself.

The dualities are what make you *whole*.

And choosing not to see, to keep this part of you in the dark, does not make this part of you nonexistent.

You cannot harness your personal power or *master* yourself without knowing and accepting all that you are.

—KJ's Guides

What you experience in a day, what experience
you awaken to in a day, is one of many happening in
your full existence.

If you choose to experience the smell of the fresh rose
as you walk past the rosebush, you will notice your senses
heightened so that you can *live* and capture that moment
in your *entire* being.

You will notice the colors vividness as your eyes glance
upon it, then its healing aroma as your sense of smell
awakens to the experience, followed by the rose's gentle
texture as you caress the petal with your sense of touch,
and so on.

While all this is happening your being is doing even more.

It is awakening to the energy this flower emits as it comes
in contact with you.

There are a multitude of experiences happening in
one moment.

What will you choose to awaken to in this moment?

What will you choose to experience in order to expand
your consciousness today?

—Leigh

Your fear of not knowing, of self-doubt, of holding on to a memory of a hurtful past in order to protect you from future pain, keeps you from experiencing in full what you wish to experience.

You have the option of opening the door and walking through bravely or keeping it shut stuck in the fear of a memory.

These are your lessons are yours and yours alone to choose.

—Leigh

Dance to the rhythm of life.

Let your heart flow to new heights and be free.

Observe as the movements of life itself gracefully sway you side to side, lift you up when you fall, and dry your tears when you cry.

You see, without each beautiful step that takes place, the dance would not be marvelous.

Set your soul free in the movement of lifes ever-changing dance steps.

Your choreographer has a masterpiece planned and if you dance with your heart your life will be the greatest encore in an ever-changing flow.

All you have to do is just open up and allow your faith to lead you through the unchained beats of love.

You are the rhythm, the beat, the orchestra, and the dancer.

You are *love*.

—Archangel Uriel

Feel your heart as it breathes the air of love.

Begin again.

Do not let sorrows of yesterday hold you back from
happiness available for you *today.*

—Leigh

Unclutter your mind, your heart, and your body from those
things that no longer serve you.

Let go of that which does not resonate with the spirit
of you.

Having a memory is one thing.

Latching on to the energy of a memory is another.

Knowing the difference will set you free.

—Leigh

You are free when you *choose* to be free, when you choose to seek out *truth,* and when you choose to step in to your *heart armor of love.*

There are many types of love, but the one you are searching for, that void you feel, is a love unconditional and free.

—Leigh

There is someone seeking your acceptance, forgiveness, and love. This person knows he/she has let you down, knows he/she has some rough flaws, and knows he/she tests you daily with *love.* This person is you. You see, if you are looking to attract better than what you have today it starts within. If you are attracting people who seem not to love you just the way you like or bring in what you considered flawed outcomes, situations, and so on, then it's time to go within and see where you are not accepting, loving, and forgiving these parts of yourself. It's time to stop blaming and lovingly assume responsibility of your life.

The light of day brings you clarity to see what you fear or have not accepted n your dark. The light of the moon brings you the ability to gently heal that which you fear by facing it

Your strengths are yours strengths.

Your weaknesses are also your strengths.

Being able to accept all of you makes you stronger than those who sees perceived weakness as failure.

Light, love, acceptance of yourself,

—Leigh

Two men were given two stones each, one black,
one white, by a stranger. When asked what they would do
with his stones, the first man said, "I only have two stones.

There is nothing I can do." The second man said,
"I will build the foundation of my home with these," and so
it became that he had the largest castle in the land.

Blessed by the gift of a stranger, the home of his heart was
made golden and the land became prosperous enough for
all to enjoy.

There will be those who wish to be around you for all of
who you are in the nakedness of your vulnerability,
and there will be those who will be around for what they
think you can offer them.

In both situations, you are given an opportunity to
choose what you will allow and what you deserve
according to you.

—Leigh

It is not what you said you would do yesterday,
but what you do today, that plants the seeds of
your tomorrows.

—Leigh

Many are scared to be alone, in silence with themselves,
so they thrive on staying busy and always needing another
to fill the void of an emptiness that can only be filled
from within.

You can only give gold when you have gold to give.

The key is in your hand will you hold tightly to it or will you
use the key that was given to you to unlock your *truth,*
your *light,* and ultimately your true nature of *love?*

Love is you and once you can see this, feel this, and know
this about yourself, so can the rest of the world.

—Leigh

Extraordinary moments are not to be searched for,
but to be made aware of in each moment.

—Leigh

Your *gift* to this world is *you* empowered.

You can only be who you know yourself to be if you accept
another's truth as your own without experiencing the
resonance of what is true to you according to soul within,
you miss a wonderful experience of life through the eyes of
the *soul* and the *heart* of mankind though you,
through your journey.

—Leigh

Your soul yearns for your connection to the pieces of you.

You do not now see in yourself, yet notice in others with admiration and awe.

So it reflects in front of you something beautiful, something special so you too can go within and know that you are the beauty of life reflected in front of you.

It could not exist within your experience if you were not a vibrational match, if it did not exist within.

—Leigh

The moment you let go of the judgments, the limitations, and the fear of illusion is the moment you set your soul on fire with the *radiance* of the eternal flame of unconditional love of one love and a world not divided, but *whole* in consciousness in peace.

We are one.

The struggle is not outside, but inside of you.

Conquer it.

—Leigh

If I humbly look you in the eyes and stare a little longer than I should, please forgive me.

I just wish to share the love that I see when I look at you, back with you, from the window of our *souls.*

You have always been love, dear ones,

—Leigh and Jesus

It takes *wisdom* to know when its time to let go, *forgiveness* to set you free, and *love*—unbreakable, pure, and divine—to know and trust that it is for the highest good.

Light love,

—Leigh

The beauty in growth is growing, stretching yourself more than you thought possible.

During these times we outgrow situations, experiences, and even people we thought were the constant in an always changing world.

Just to learn the real constant is the connection you will have forever through the strings of the heart with each individual experience through the travels of your *soul's* journey.

Light love always connected,

—Leigh

Without endings, there can be no *rebirths*.

Without rebirths, there can be no *new* experiences
to show you how *extraordinarily* great and divine your
essence is.

You are love.

Light love,

—Leigh

You are all you seek to be and become, *within*.

The way to bring yourself to this place is by turning the light
switch on inside.

Tap into your omnipresence.

Light love,

—Leigh

A rose is beautiful, yet is capable of pricking.

The sun shines a beautiful ray of light, yet it has the capability to scorch.

We are divinely beautiful beings with amazing gifts, yet we shut ourselves off to our greatness by choosing to follow the words of another.

There exists within each of us opposite a polar of our self.

You can choose to deny all of the aspects that make up *you* by pretending that parts of you do not exist, but if you do you will fail yourself.

You say you come to succeed?

Well, then you must know what success is and where it resides in you, in all of *you*.

—Leigh

Is the mind more consciously aware that stares at a grain of sand and sees a grain of sand or the mind that sees the grain of sand as a starting point?

Some minds see many possibilities to create something amazing, more conscious.

Have you taken the time to reassess your life lately?

Sometime our focus is so much on the future that we do not take the time to see how our lives have changed from our yesterdays, thus we're skipping the step of gratification and fast forwarding to what we want for the future.

Do we take enough time to realize that today, this moment, is the future written by our yesterdays?

You can only cherish moments when you live them and realize you took another step forward to get here to your today.

Yesterday's future is now.

Take a moment and have gratitude.

Light, love, gratitude,

—Leigh

Can you lead the world with eyes and mind half open?

Can you lead a household whose foundation is not solid?

Can you lead *yourself* when your heart is not ready?

Leading begins with leading yourself without waiver,
without doubt in what you believe in.

—Leigh

Not to be fooled, a person who gives with his/her heart
and not his/her mind is not naive.

Quite the contrary.

Not to be fooled, a person who smiles to your face while
you laugh and talk behind his/her back is not naive.

You are very mistaken.

This person compassionately understands his/her lesson
in these situations, and therefore rewarded with a victory,
mastery.

He/she is untouched by those with foul intent.

—Leigh

Sometimes eyes wide open appear as eyes shut closed.

Perception of the mind vs. perception of the heart.

—Leigh

The journey is about the journey of you.

Attempting to match a moment with that of anyone else outside of you will lead to self-defeat.

You have one journey, one self, one moment to make it all worthwhile and remarkable.

When you realize that the best you can be is you at your best in each divine moment, you will be in the flow of your own magnificence.

And that is a gift incomparable to anyone that you may admire or idolize.

You have your own greatness to shine and share.

Step into your footsteps and not the shadows of another.

—Leigh

We sometimes feel the need to explain the whats and whys of our lives.

Your life needs no explanation.

Just live your life fully and be true to your authentic self.

Those who are there for your journey will be there no matter what, and those who are there for other motives will naturally fall away.

False light cannot stay hidden and true light cannot be put out.

—Leigh

If we aspire to be who were are instead of who we think we should want to be, a level of victory of the self is achieved.

You were created as perfect as the *one* who created you.

You only need to open your consciousness, your heart and your eyes, to experience your wholeness.

—Archangel Uriel

Fighting against a natural flow of a current may make you stronger physically, but going with the natural flow will make you stronger as a whole.

You will bend, you will shift, but you will not break.

—Archangel Uriel

If we stand still for even just five minutes in a day,
we *allow* a current to flow through us and move us gently
on the paths we are destined to be on.

—Archangel Uriel

Without the eye of the heart we are unable to see the true
connections we have to one another, to *all*,
and to understand that we are really not that different from
each other.

Our life choices still bring us each back to the beginning,
to our truth as a whole to oneness.

—Archangel Uriel

In the chalice of our hearts we find the courage to move forward, the strength to face obstacles, and the love to accept, forgive, and heal a world that is ready for the next chapter: the next stage of a grand and free way of living and being.

—Leigh

Each person will bring an aspect of you out that needs your attention to resolve heal and love.

—Leigh

Children play in innocence with attention given to the
moment of what is directly in front of them.

It is because of this that they will conquer all that comes
before them.

Their energy is focused on the now and they are led by the
heart of their own judgment.

This allows them the freedom to imagine envision and
create right here in now a world that an adult, seeing
through adult eyes, cannot begin to understand until they
themselves reach deep inside and connect to a part of
themselves still very alive and wondrous,
ready to take them to the next level through cooperation of
the inner child and adult in unification reconnect as one.

—Leigh

You can see, but not fully understand.

You can feel, but not know.

You can love a love, but not *love* in the highest love.

Without knowing who you are and where you've been,
and without accessing the grace of forgiveness for
yourself and others, you won't be able to open yourself to
experience your journey a thousand times over through the
perception of that which is higher than you know yourself
to be and less than you would ever expect to be.

—Leigh

Through you I come to know myself.

Through me you will come to know yourself.

I exist in you.

You exist in me.

We are one, we are love.

—Leigh

My heart stands naked in front of you.

My words are stripped to their most simplistic form.

I stand before you not without a past, not without flaws,
but as a complete being here in transparency of
my vulnerability.

—Leigh

We have chosen our paths, our ways of existing and being.

When what is not working has been for as long as it has, there is the need for new choices to be made.

You cannot clear the clutter if you are traveling the same path in circles.

You must be willing to take a chance on a new path, a new way, even if fear rests inside of you.

By facing the fear of change and what is currently unknown to you, you will come to vanish fear and come into a resilient omnipresent love.

You choose your path and it will remain your path until you choose a better path to travel.

—Leigh

You cannot experience life fully without feeling and being the experiences that you choose.

You want the pain to go away, but when the feeling confronts you, you run and hide.

You want the memories you have resting in the back of your mind to disappear, but when they pop up for healing, forgiveness, and resolve you push them aside.

You cannot let go of something you are not willing to face and you cannot be the person you are meant to be if you hold tightly to the person you were.

—Leigh

You smile the most angelic of smiles.

If only they knew the millennium of tears that made this smile so.

Your words spoken so elegantly poetic.

If only they knew the history that made this so.

You move so gracefully carefree.

If only they knew the movements that transpired transforming these movements into its grace.

You make life and love sound so easy.

If only they knew the fight for life and the battle of self-love you had to endure.

If only they knew.

—Leigh

The distance is shorter than the time it takes you to contemplate your move.

Time is of the essence and the only way to move is by faith.

You are more than what you know and more than what you may ever know.

But the chance is given to you freely to come to know the magnificence you are made of, the magnificence that you are.

Are you ready to allow yourself to feel at your most vulnerable state is to receive at your highest state?

And this is where the fear, the doubt, the worry subsides and *love fulfills.*

—God/Source

You see, your heart is already filled with the life support
of *love*.

Fill your mind with love and this spreads into your cells,
your blood, your body, your work, life experiences,
and more.

You already are, so just *be*.

—Leigh

A canopy of love always surrounds you, its presence fills
you, so sit still long enough to let it move you, sway you,
shape you, and fulfill you authentically.

—Archangels

The strength is not outside of you, but inside.

Courage is not mind over matter, but heart over
the circumstances.

Vision is not shown to you, yet understood by you with the
trust of your inner wisdom and light.

The capacity and capability of who you are supersedes the
expansion of what you have been taught.

—Archangels

How can you live a life scripted by the spectators of your life?

How can you break free if you are too afraid to touch the chains that bind you?

How can you say you know how to give love when it's given conditionally?

How can you say you have trust when you won't take the time to see your false fear is unjustified?

How can you come to know me when all you see is echoes of hers from your past?

—Leigh

By choosing to focus and find the beauty, the positive, and the love in others and situations does not mean one does not acknowledge the polarities in this existence.

In an era where we have come into an ability to create and cocreate, energy is better spent focused on what is in front of our eyes and what is possible to create and recreate for the betterment of all.

I choose not to be blinded to all that is and accept for me in these moments my focus is co-creating through eyes and a vision of love.

—Archangel Ariel

It is my destiny to think not as you have taught me or even as you deem correct, but to breathe into existence thoughts that come from within myself.

I am both the master and the student of my chosen path

—Leigh

I chose to fall so that you could learn that victory is not in always being able to stand tall but in falling and getting back up resiliently and stronger than ever centered in the heart.

I chose the rocky road instead of the smooth terrain, so that you could see how the rocks toughened my stance in each step taken in truth, in light.

I chose to love through the lies, deception, and broken promises to show you that hatred, anger, revenge are not the way.

Compassion, not judgment, love, not anger will bring a resolution.

This will bring you to experience a love of the highest degree.

You are not the illusion, but the resolution to the battle you seek to end, inside of you.

—Jesus and Archangel Ariel

How do you teach and lead without forcing?

You *guide*.

How do you give love to a heart so badly scarred?

Without expectations.

How do you come to a place of knowing?

You trust with all that you are.

—Leigh

The perfect words needed to speak are spoken from the heart and written with the ink of *love*.

—Leigh

Do not be quick to judge, they are only mirrors of you asking to be addressed.

Do not be quick to blame when the responsibility resides in you.

Do not be quick to throw stones when stones, like boomerangs, ricochet back.

Do not be quick to tell another what he/she is doing is wrong, when the path the person walks was made for him/her and not you.

There exist experiences and people not meant for you to fully understand but only to observe for a larger picture of what your eyes and ego cannot understand unless through the vibration of *true, divine, unconditional love.*

—Soul

The best competition for you, competition that's readily available, is the side of you that you have been putting off facing due to fear.

Defeat the part of you that you choose to hide and you will gain an army worth of strength, courage, victory all in the man of *one*.

—Leigh

Are you listening?

The bird chirped at you as you walked by.

Did you hear it?

Are you *listening*?

The stranger just gave you a sincere compliment as you
turned your head in judgment of their looks.

Did you hear it?

Are you listening?

Your heart weeps for the love of self you need because
this is where your vitality lies.

Did you hear it?

Are you listening?

Did you hear it?

Or is the noise of your mind and life getting in the way of
the soft-spoken messages and answers you seek?

—Soul

You have to get through your weaknesses to find
your strengths.

You have be alone to understand the importance of a
team united.

You have to face your fear to walk in valor.

You have to open your heart to understand the depth of
a love that is whole, that is all encompassing and divine
by nature.

—Soul

Don't forget the people you've encountered along the way,
as they are your biggest teachers and cheerleaders.

Don't forget the importance of your words,
as they echo in the mind forever.

Don't forget who you are and why you are, as the
existence of your authenticity depends on it.

Don't forget love is in the moment and you are
that moment.

—Leigh

The gift of life is found inside of you.

There is no circumstance or person who can bring you to
the place of wholeness or love.

When you stop searching you allow what already is to
show itself to you and just *be*.

—Archangels

Once you tap into to this internally you will have gained the
gift of gifts.

All that you seek outside of you is inside of you.

Come to know the world in which you exist form the inside
looking out.

—Archangels

There can be many voices speaking to you all at once
telling you who or what you should do or be.

But the only voice that matters is the one speaking from
your soul, your spirit. It already knows your path and holds
your *key.*

—Archangels

Sure there are distractions along the way.

They teach you to focus on the goal right in front of you
unwavering with determination and the will to see it straight
to the end.

—Leigh

The task is not to get through each day but to genuinely
live each day fully from moment to moment.

To find happiness through the strife, through the sadness,
is to find happiness infinitely through all moments of time.

—Leigh

You fell down, not because you were unworthy,
but because you deserved more than what you were in
that moment and the only way to show you that you were
more was to humbly break you and allow you to remake
you into the king or queen you were destined to be.

—Jesus

There are the beliefs created by man and there are the
beliefs connected by *oneness* consciousness.

You will follow what you are ready and open to believing.

The truth detector to any of these beliefs and what
resonates with you authentically will be found in your heart.

—RR's Guides

You search for the light in the darkness from behind, from your past.

The light is *within* you, now, in the present moment.

If you cannot stand still and just be where you are in the here, in *now,* how can you expect to see the opportunities right within your reach?

If you cannot let go how you can let in?

Your fear is an illusion.

Face it, confront it, *love* it, and let it go.

Right now this moment is the future.

Give your best and be your best!

Your *light* will overcome.

—Leigh

Follow the way of your heart.

There lies your true *potential,* true existence, and your true being, which is naturally connected to all.

—Soul

You are rejecting a part of you that makes you whole.

That makes you, *you.*

Shut eyes may shut you off from what you wish not to see in the world but they cannot shut you off from what you must see, and learn to *love* about yourself.

—God/Source

Can you see that what you question that comes from the mouths of others is there to challenge who you are and help you define what you stand for?

Can you hear your soul as its words echo through your being to let you know who you are and help you define what you stand for?

Can you feel as your heart opens to love and closes to the pain, just to reopen up in forgiveness and let love flow as it should to let you know who you are and help you define what you stand for?

—God/Source

You cannot separate the matrix of a continual oneness and an undeniable love that connects us all to each other and each other to the *divine*.

—God/Source

Love's fight is one worth fighting, you don't ever really lose,
you *gain.*

What do you gain, you might ask?

Well, do you remember who you were before love's battle
and know who you are as a result?

You chose experiences to make you better, to make
you more aware of who you are and the importance of a
greater love—one worth fighting for and one that changes
and shifts you through *growth* of choices.

The fight for love will bring you to know love.

A love deeper than the mind knows on its own and purer
than the eyes alone can see.

There is no wrong choice to knowing love, just steps,
just movements in each moment that is right for you and
your journey back to the truth, back to love.

—God/Source and Jesus

Playing the violin, you realize that different strings are
different notes making different sound.

Hearing the violin as it's played, you realize different sounds
or melodies will come from stroking different strings.

Both views and perspectives are right depending on where
you are in relation to the violin.

In a certain order, a glorious sound is heard and felt.

It makes no difference if you are playing the violin yourself
or hearing the melodies as the strings are stroked.

You are still involved still connected by the one thing that
holds you both together.

Every person, place, and situation plays a role to make the
whole complete and the frequency available.

— Pleiadians

The distance between you and where you wish to be is not far. It is where you hold your attention/vision that makes it appear so.

Where is your focus?

On your fears or on your goals?

—Leigh

Playing it safe does not promise you security.

It keeps you holding on to something that is meant for you to let go of and emerge from.

Playing whole heartedly, trusting, and risking, however, will bring you to the security of knowing you have what it takes to *live* it, *dream* it and *be* it authentically with no regrets.

—Leigh

You have drive, but do you have ambition to achieve?

You have the force, the will, to do what it takes, but do you have the *passion* needed?

Does it resonate with your heart?

If so, stop holding yourself back up in life?

Press play and move forward steadfastly after your dreams.

—Leigh

Diving into the ocean you are able to see and interact with all its creatures and the habitat that exists there.

There might be a few creatures you need to maneuver yourself around to successfully reach the ocean floor, but it's both worth it and necessary.

You are able to choose what you take with you to your destination, what to let go of and what is only for the simple pleasure of viewing.

The path is yours and you always choose.

You always choose.

—Leigh

That smile is beautiful and what makes it so is the life lived that can be seen by looking into your eyes.

See, even if I cannot see your journey, your smile lets me know where you are now and where you will be tomorrow.

The story of a smile.

—Leigh

Stepping onto solid ground makes you feel safe and secure, while stepping on a muddy, cracked, or what appears unstable ground may have you feeling unsure.

Both offer opportunities of a foundation.

The difference is one was built there before you by another for others to follow and the other allows you to build your own solid foundation according to your gifts, your path, your light and your effort.

—God/Source

Dance to the heartbeat of life as you move through it.

Embrace it, love it, because it is through living you find yourself, come to know yourself and love yourself.

—Soul

We fail not because there were no opportunities to take but because we did not see those opportunities because they were not packaged to our liking.

We did not seize the opportunities because fear of not knowing what would happen stood between us and our dream.

The blame is not on the outer world but your inner world.

Changes, views, perceptions, and a recalibration of limiting beliefs need your attention, *inside*.

It is your outer world that reflects your inner world.

This battle is yours and is won within.

—Leigh

You have great expectations from this life, but do you put
out high expectation results in the lives of others.

You have everything in this world to gain by giving to others
what you yourself expect.

You are love and greatness, but until you can feel see
and believe this about yourself you will always be your
biggest hindrance.

—Leigh

Until you are able to open you mind, your eyes,
and your heart to experience what you desire in life without
limiting boundaries and judgments of how it should be,
you will stand still, just wanting, just waiting.

—Leigh

If you continue to run you will continue to tire and wear
yourself down.

It is when you finally stop, say enough is enough, and face
what you fear that you step into victory and fear falls away.

The cycle ends when you stop running and trust in who
you are to conquer any obstacle.

You take charge of the cycle or it takes charge of you.

—Leigh

To fall is to be broken.

To cry is to feel within the depths of your soul.

To let go is to be… in freedom of life lived wholly.

—Leigh

You will grow and you will change because of it.

Though people and places may change, love will remain the same.

If you so choose to stay in this center, you will have clarity of the bigger picture.

The little lessons and choices affect us all as a whole, all as *one*.

What separates you is the same tie that keeps you connected.

Whether you view from the mountaintop or view from the ocean floor, the story—the picture—is still the same, you just have different views that regulate what you see and how you see it.

—Archangels

There is a beauty to be noticed in the sky at different times of day.

But only if you choose to aim your sight for the skies can you have a chance at seeing it.

There will be those who can only handle what is directly in front of them and there will be those who can handle what is in front of them, behind, below, and above them.

Those are the ones who will come to discover just what the sky and all that surrounds it is composed of.

They will come to know the unrestricted truth of all.

—Archangels

You shed a tear because they do not understand
who you are.

Stop, they cannot understand who they themselves are,
let alone another.

You shed a tear because you must defend a truth that
needs no defense.

Stop, truth needs no back up.

Its power cannot be denied.

You shed a tear because you know they lack a love within
and wish to change this for them.

Stop.

The love is needed only within you, for this is the only place
to change and better another through the change and love
you give yourself.

—Archangels

To conform to the words of another . . . The muse.

To accept that which you do not understand without
questioning . . . The Muse.

To feel and be as lived through an outsider's vision . . . The
Muse.

You will always be the Muse until you step into the shoes
of yourself, authentically, uniquely and lovingly.

—Leigh

It's only mysticism until you yourself walk the journey of
what has been labeled unknown.

Then you realize there was only a mystery because no one
chooses to walk the long walk due to fear.

—Leigh

We learn to find our center in any environment once we learn to quiet the noise thrown out there to knock us off of balance.

—Leigh

Love's footsteps walk alone until we learn to carry and balance of love within.

When we are ready, the wings of love attach to lift us higher and spread that love outside of us.

We never lose love, we just choose to change our focus to something else.

Love is love and love knows no different than love itself.

—Archangel Chamuel

There is a lot of love you have to give.

Your very existence is love.

Speak it from your mouth.

Be it with your heart.

Live it with each breath.

Drown fears and worries and crank up the volume of love.

It is you within and throughout.

—Archangel Chamuel

You have the wings to set yourself free,
the key to unlock doors,
and the spirit to do all things grand.

—Natives

The focus is not on another's perception of you but the perception you have of yourself.

Let not another's words or actions discourage you from the truth and light that you are.

Their thoughts are not yours to mold and conquer to attain success.

Your thoughts and actions mastered in love through all circumstances people and places will amount to your own true success.

—Archangels

This I speak is true.

The branch that is broken into two pieces did not break
because it was weak.

Rather, the power, the message, that the branch held
was so relevant and direly needed it need to be shared
between two bearers.

Two different people on two different journeys would
spread its message of light into this world because they
would come across two different types of people needing
to know the true message of strength, of love.

But the message is the same.

Its light the same.

We are one.

—God/Source

Rain down sweet joy.

Lift my spirit with your words, ease my mind with your melody, and drown my heart with the flow of your music.

—Leigh

A harvest is given to you this day.

Some may see only a harvest of one where others will see a harvest of many.

But it is still harvest.

Are you grateful for what you have harvested?

No matter how little it is still plentiful to the heart that sees the value of a seed at its fruition.

—Natives

In this moment you choose circumstance over moment.

Choose moment over circumstances and you will
conquer your inner world and anything thrown at you in
your outer world.

—Archangel Uriel

There are chambers in your *heart* that allow you to get to
know your *true* self authentically.

Inside you will find the keys to your destined life,
your latent gifts, and you will experience a *love* of a lifetime.

This will be the love you share with the world.

—Archangels

The gift is not found in what you give somebody,
but in what they find in themselves and about themselves
as a result of what you have presented them.

—Archangels

A rebirth of any kind requires you coming to grips with, and
accepting that which is being transformed and reborn.

You go through rebirth because you have now advanced
passed the level you are currently at.

You have to allow yourself to shed old skin to see the
illuminated brighter thicker and fuller skin you have now
grown into.

—Archangels

In this moment you choose circumstance over moment.

Choose moment over circumstances and you will conquer your inner world and anything thrown at you in your outer world.

—Archangel Uriel

There are chambers in your *heart* that allow you to get to know your *true* self authentically.

Inside you will find the keys to your destined life, your latent gifts, and you will experience a *love* of a lifetime.

This will be the love you share with the world.

—Archangels

The gift is not found in what you give somebody,
but in what they find in themselves and about themselves
as a result of what you have presented them.

—Archangels

A rebirth of any kind requires you coming to grips with, and
accepting that which is being transformed and reborn.

You go through rebirth because you have now advanced
passed the level you are currently at.

You have to allow yourself to shed old skin to see the
illuminated brighter thicker and fuller skin you have now
grown into.

—Archangels

Light is all around you and within you.

But if your eyes are only focused on the darkness in a room, in your life and you choose not to budge or relax even just a little, then your eyes cannot perceive much more of anything else.

When you decide to relax your focus, to open your field of view and expand just a smidgen more, that tiny light has the freedom to show you more and to light the entire room, your entire path.

But only when you are ready and open to a frequency of more.

—Archangels

I have no limits, so please stop trying to confine me.

I *am* love.

I have no motive, so please stop second guessing me.

I *am* love.

I have no desire to hide from you, so please stop
searching for me outside.

I *am* within, I am everywhere.

I *am* love.

—Quan Yin

Strength is who you are as a result of each choice
you choose.

Strength is measured by heart.

Strength is love.

—Leigh

The greatest jewel is finding your strength in love and through love.

—Archangels

There are paths laid out in front of you and choices you must make to stay on that path or to begin a new path.

There is no one who makes those final choices, but you.

You will walk through a beautiful garden of flowers and pull yourself through traitorous waters, all because it is on your path to greatness.

It is your path to greatness and back to your essence of *love*.

—Archangel Chamuel

Playing it safe does not guarantee you safety.

Playing for keeps does not gain you forever.

Playing to win does not promise you a victory.

Playing for love will bring you one step closer to the
greatest who ever lived, and more so, to the greatest you
yourselves are destined to become.

—Archangel Uriel

Each person has a story to tell like a living, breathing book
in motion.

If you have not taken the time to read the chapters,
and chose to go by the appearance of the cover as you
would look at it upon a shelf, you will never know what the
story is about.

Do not judge what you fear or don't understand based on
a distant visual of what you see.

—Leigh

The present, the now, will bring you to your dreams.

Looking back will only get you stuck and out of range for what is ahead for you.

You are offered an opportunity to either repair or replace the broken string in your violin as it sits waiting to be played.

If you choose to repair the string, the music it once played will not be the same, it will not be perfectly in tune.

If you choose to let go of the attachment to the string and replace it, the melody will match the original if not exceed it.

Tend to your instrument and your instrument finely tuned will play you a masterpiece

—Angels of Mercy

Sometimes there will be those who come into our lives to teach us a lesson that is painful.

There will be those who come into our lives to throw dirt on our names out of sheer spite.

There will be those who come into our lives to light our hearts afire.

Surrounding yourself with those who wish you well in your life and who give you unconditional love leaves no room for the untruths of word or actions spoken of another.

There is both a beauty and art of letting go with love.

Master yourself and you won't have room for the games, drama, or false words spoken.

—Leigh

The present, the now, will bring you to your dreams.

Looking back will only get you stuck and out of range for what is ahead for you.

You are offered an opportunity to either repair or replace the broken string in your violin as it sits waiting to be played.

If you choose to repair the string, the music it once played will not be the same, it will not be perfectly in tune.

If you choose to let go of the attachment to the string and replace it, the melody will match the original if not exceed it.

Tend to your instrument and your instrument finely tuned will play you a masterpiece

—Angels of Mercy

Sometimes there will be those who come into our lives to teach us a lesson that is painful.

There will be those who come into our lives to throw dirt on our names out of sheer spite.

There will be those who come into our lives to light our hearts afire.

Surrounding yourself with those who wish you well in your life and who give you unconditional love leaves no room for the untruths of word or actions spoken of another.

There is both a beauty and art of letting go with love.

Master yourself and you won't have room for the games, drama, or false words spoken.

—Leigh

A FINAL WORD

Well, there it is. You now know a little more about me than you did before, and more importantly you have gained some tools to aid you in your personal journey. Thank you for taking the time to sit in on this meditation from my world as seen through the eyes of love.

My prayer for you going forward is this: May you awaken to your beauty and your power, and to the highest vibration that will ever exist and coexist as your ally: love. I leave you my legacy, now leave this world yours.

LightLoveOneness,

Leigh Hickombottom

ACKNOWLEDGMENTS

Sam, thank you for teaching me to stand in my power and heal myself and this world with my light. For your constant reminder of my mission in life, I thank you as well. You have always been there for me through it all and accepted me totally as is, and I will be forever grateful for you.

Fans: Thank you for following my journey throughout the years and growing and changing along with me. I am honored to have you all as a part of my journey this life. Stay inspired. There's more to come!

RESOURCES

....

Visit Leigh's Website

LeighHickombottom.com

Connect with Leigh on the Social Networks

Facebook: www.facebook.com/1leighhickombottom

Twitter: www.twitter.com/leighHbotom

LinkedIn: www.linkedin.com/leighhickombottom

Instagram: www.instagram.com/leighhickombottom

YouTube: www.youtube.com/leighhickombottom

Invite Leigh to Speak at Your Event

Please contact at leigh@leighhickombottom.com.

ABOUT THE AUTHOR

Leigh Hickombottom is a fitness model, author, speaker, and mother. As a model, she has been featured in magazines such as *Oxygen* and *Muscle & Fitness Hers,* among others. In addition to her memoir *And Still I Smile,* Leigh is the author of two previous books on weight loss and fitness: *Logistics of Leanness* and *Logistics of Leanness Defined.* In her books she shares keys from her success on how to achieve your desired weight loss for good by using the power of the mind. Leigh also writes regular articles on her blog focusing on health and happiness.

Leigh was born in the state of Mississippi and raised in Texas. Currently she lives in Florida with her children and has planted roots there. Fitness is her area of interest and passion. Fitness is a way of life for Leigh, and maintaining her weight and physique are an important part of that lifestyle. Leigh aids different charities that make it their mission to help those in need.